I0510355

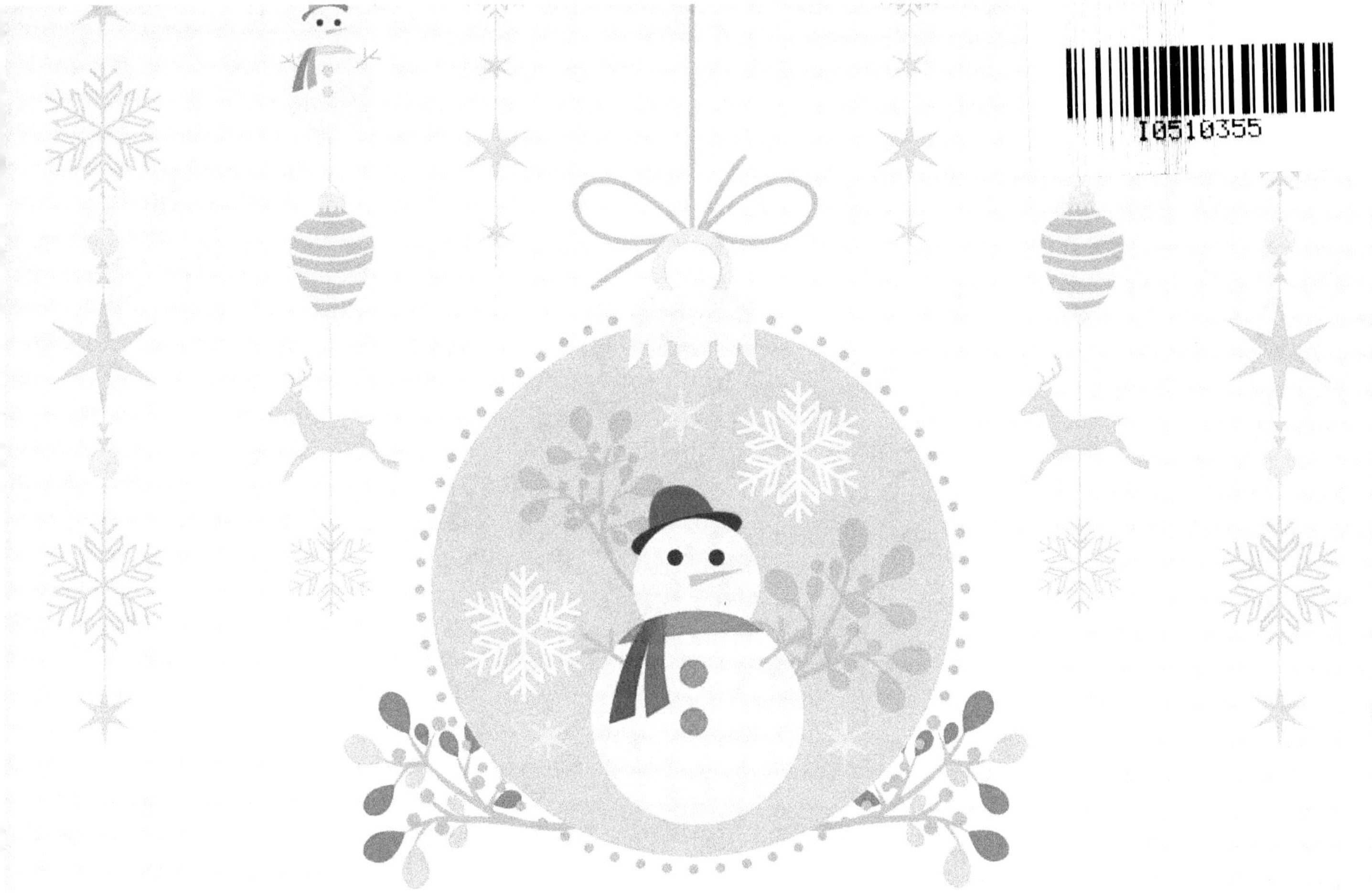

Merry

CHRISTMAS

This Books Belongs To

....

....

....

....

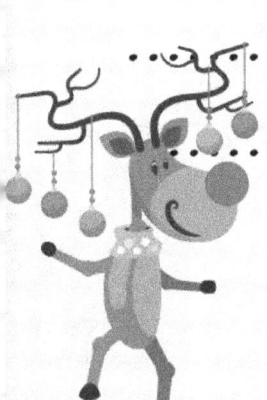

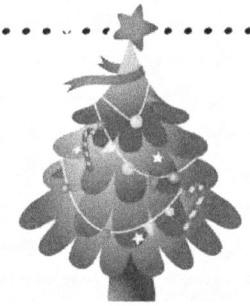

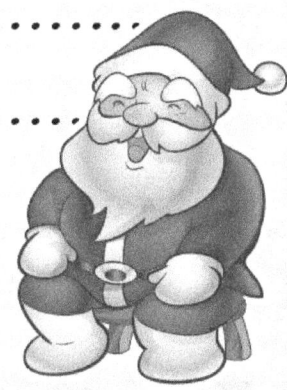

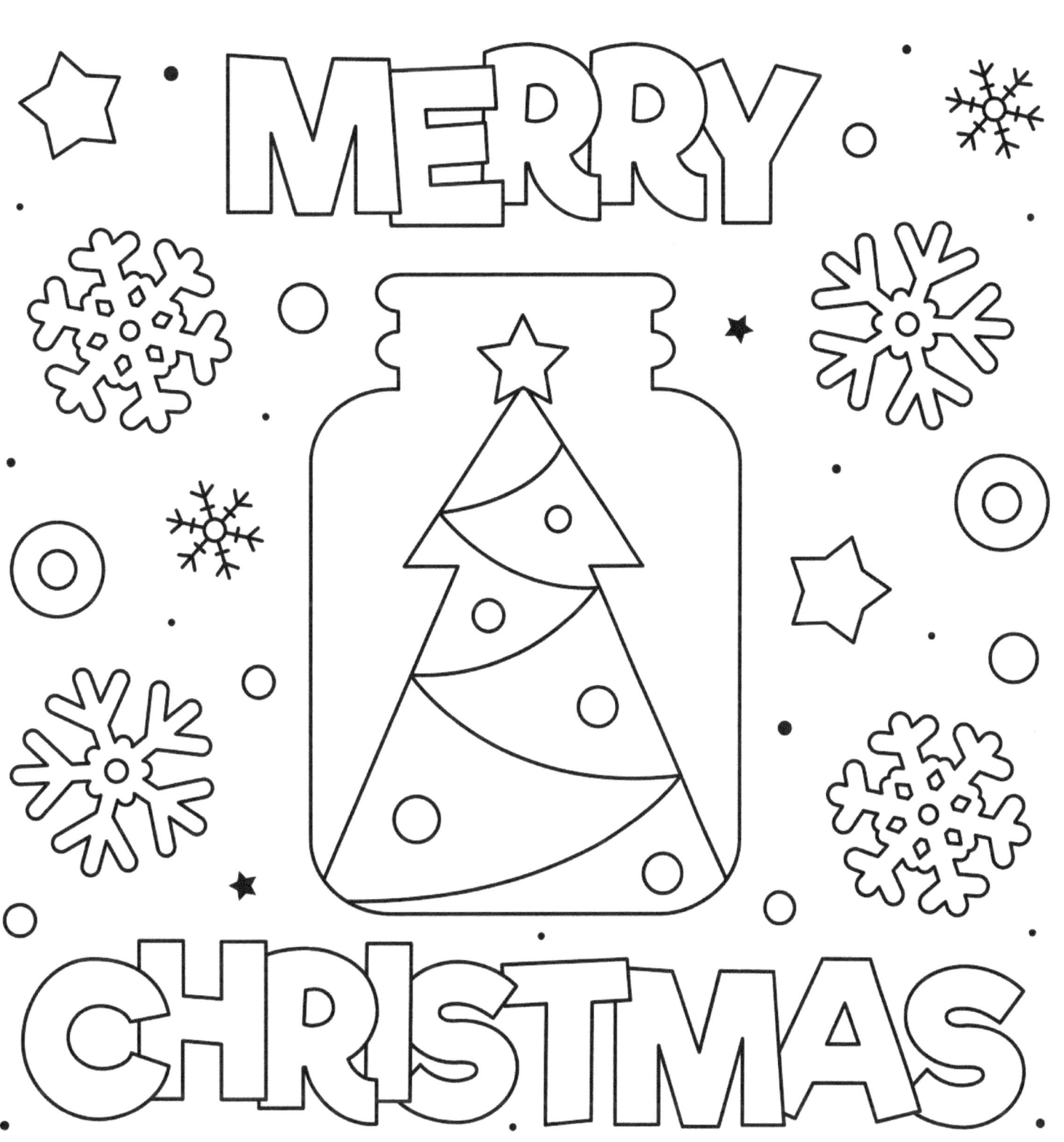

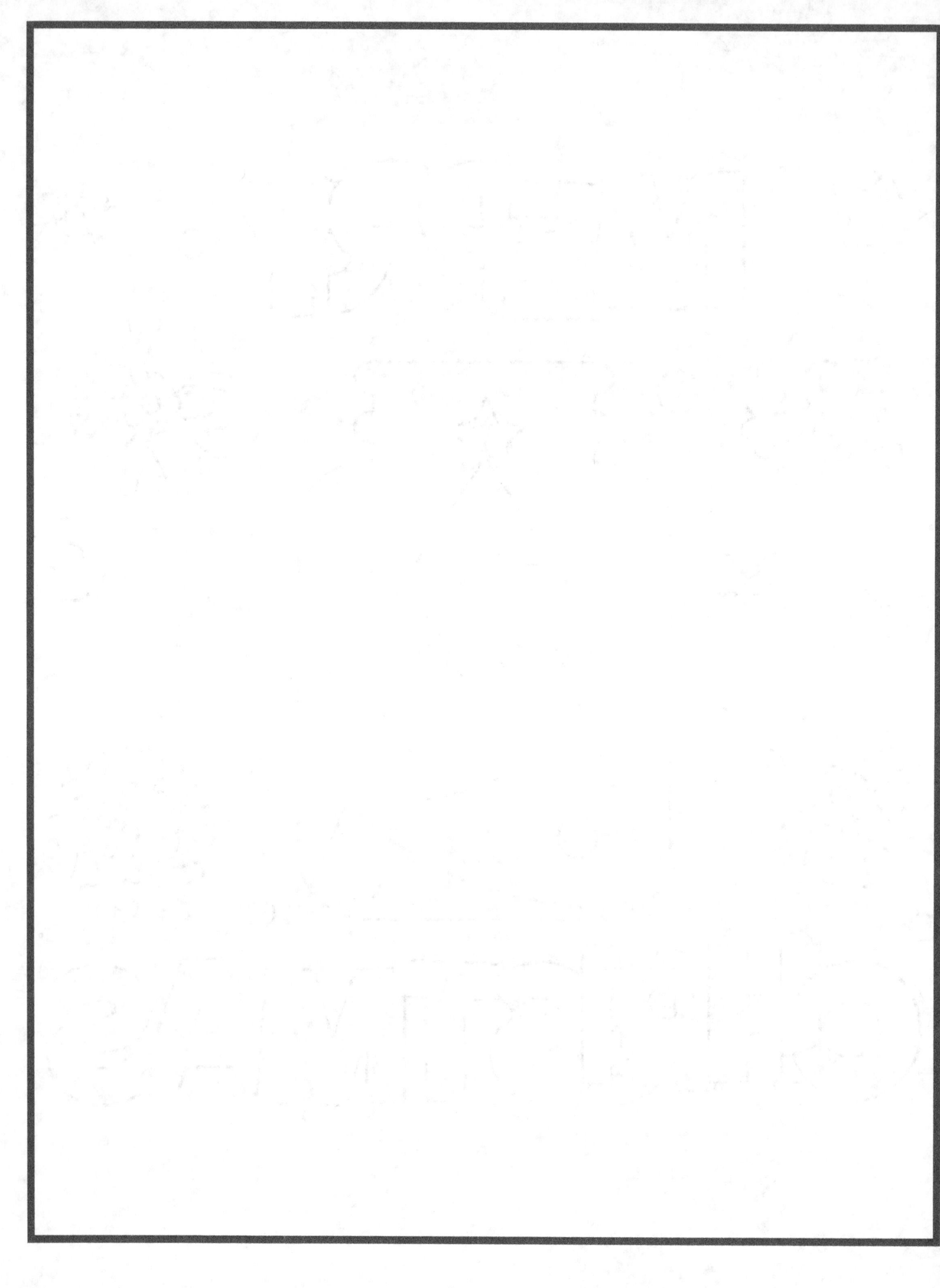

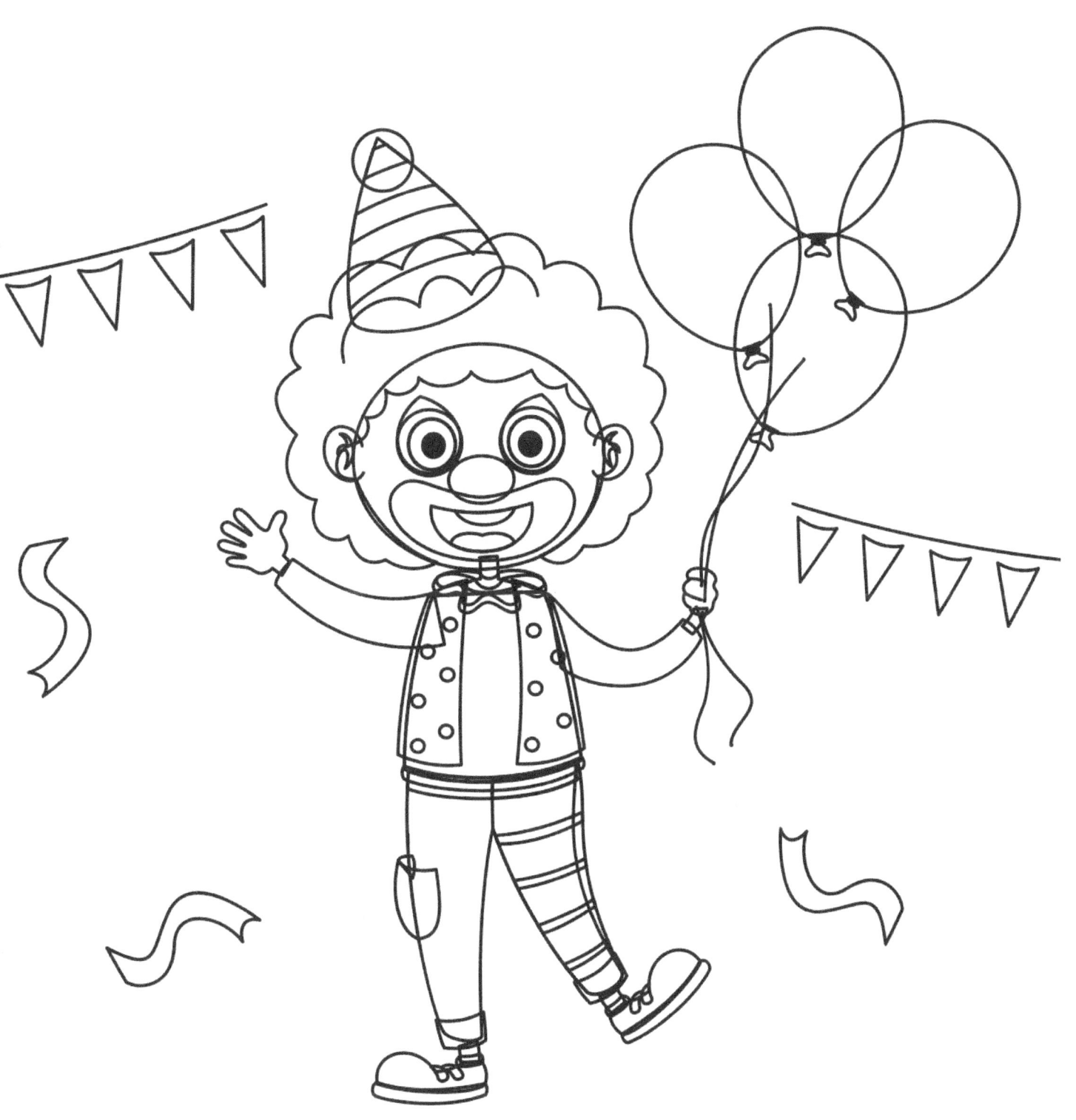

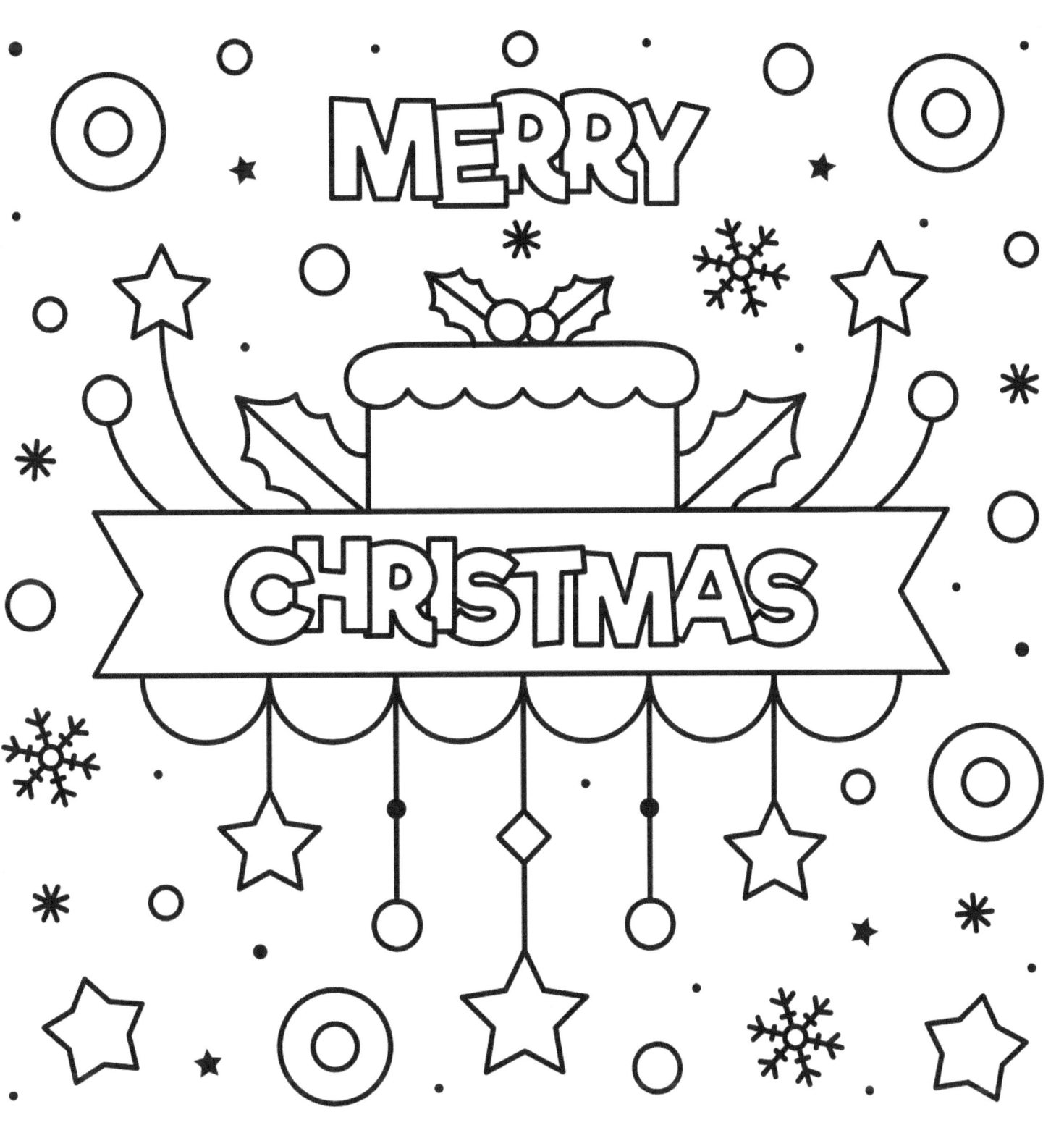

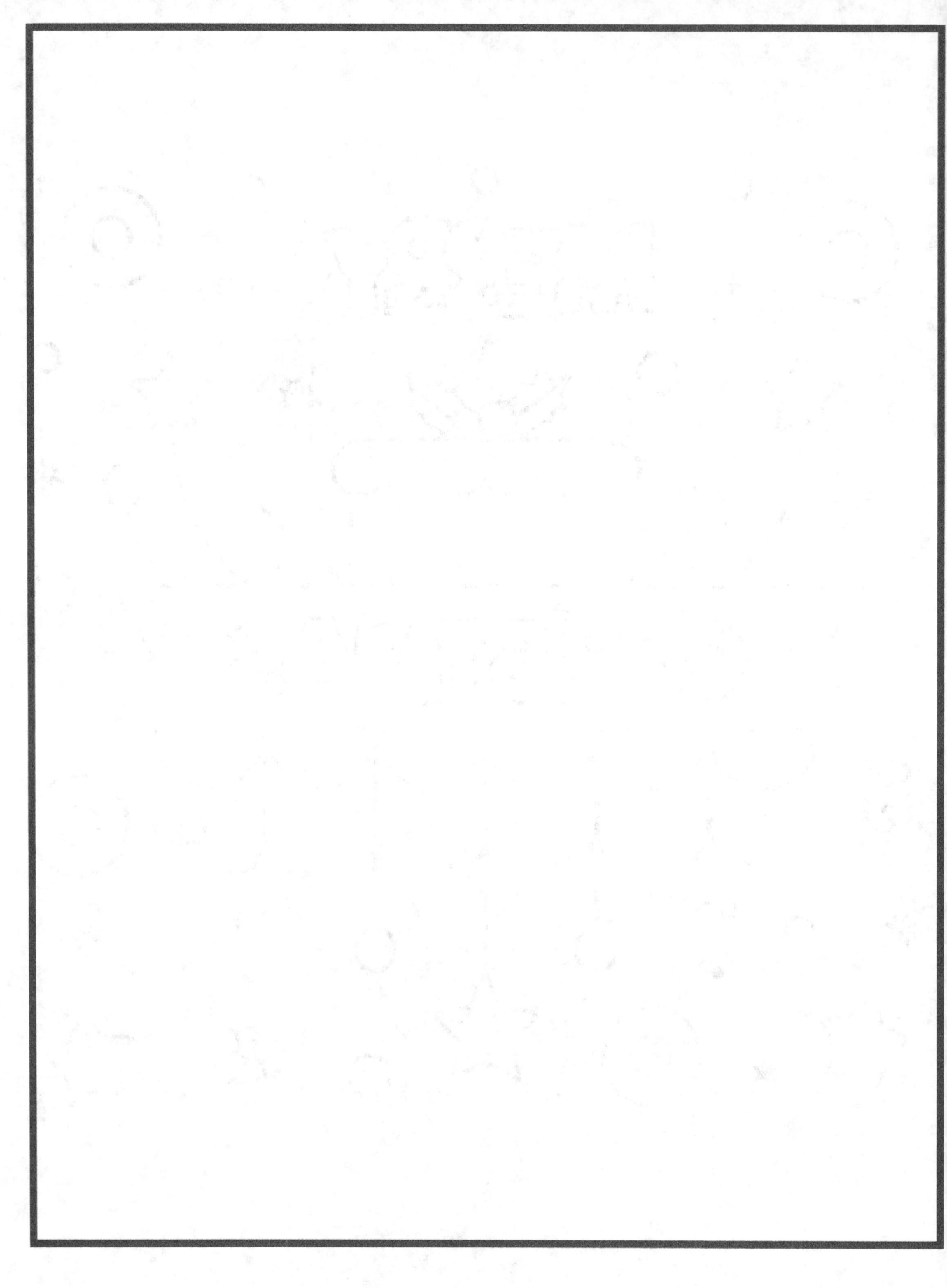

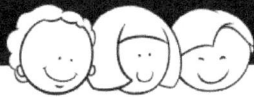 

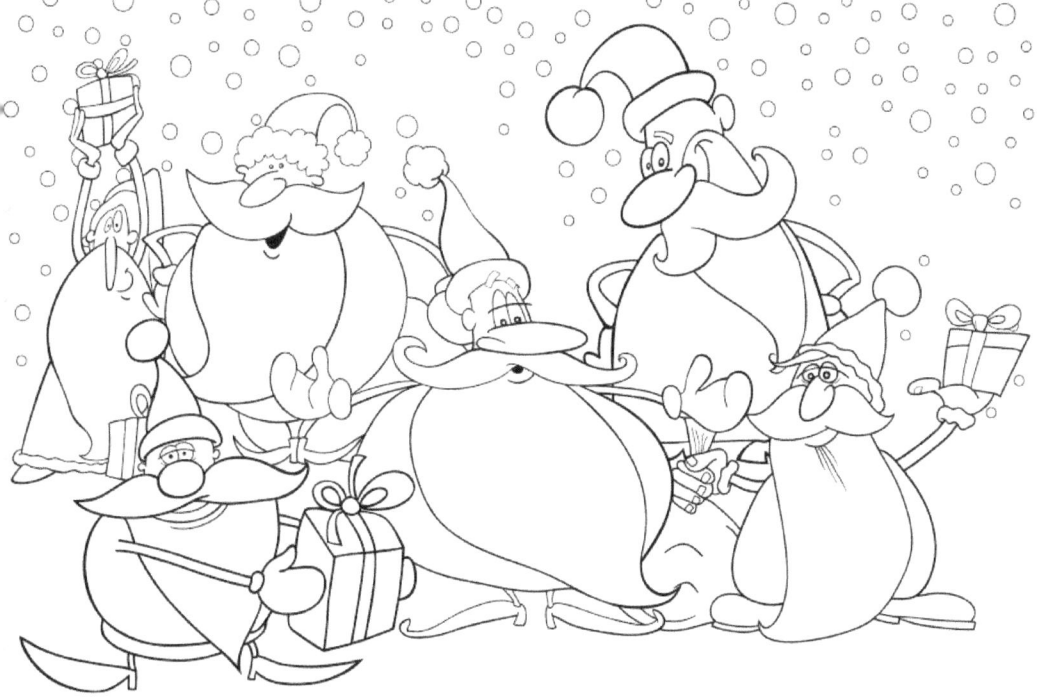

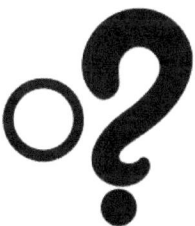

FIND
7
DIFFERENCES

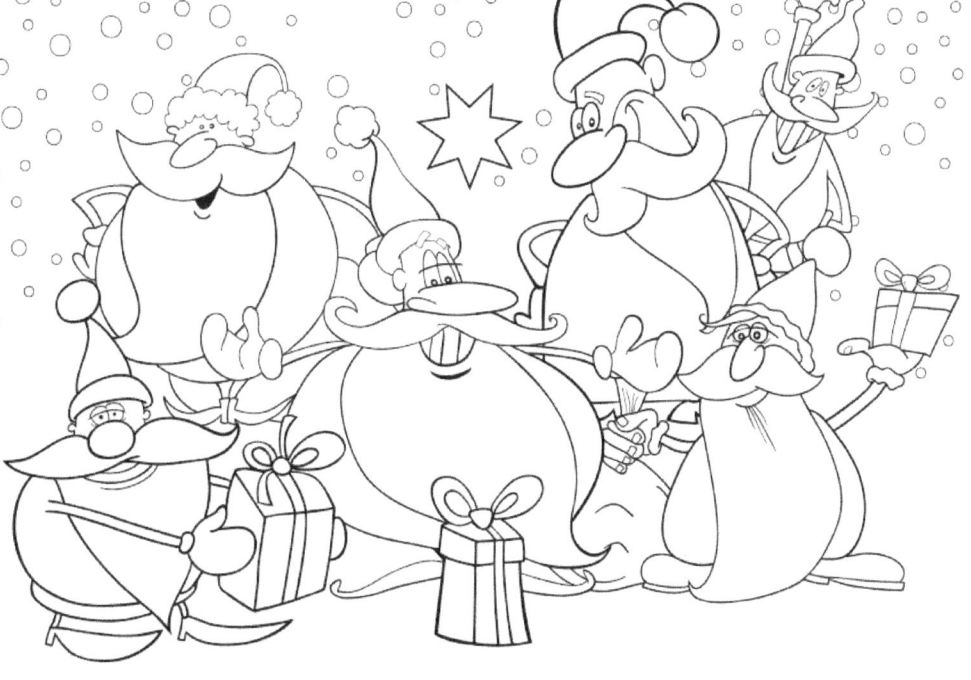

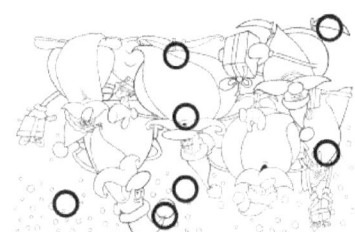

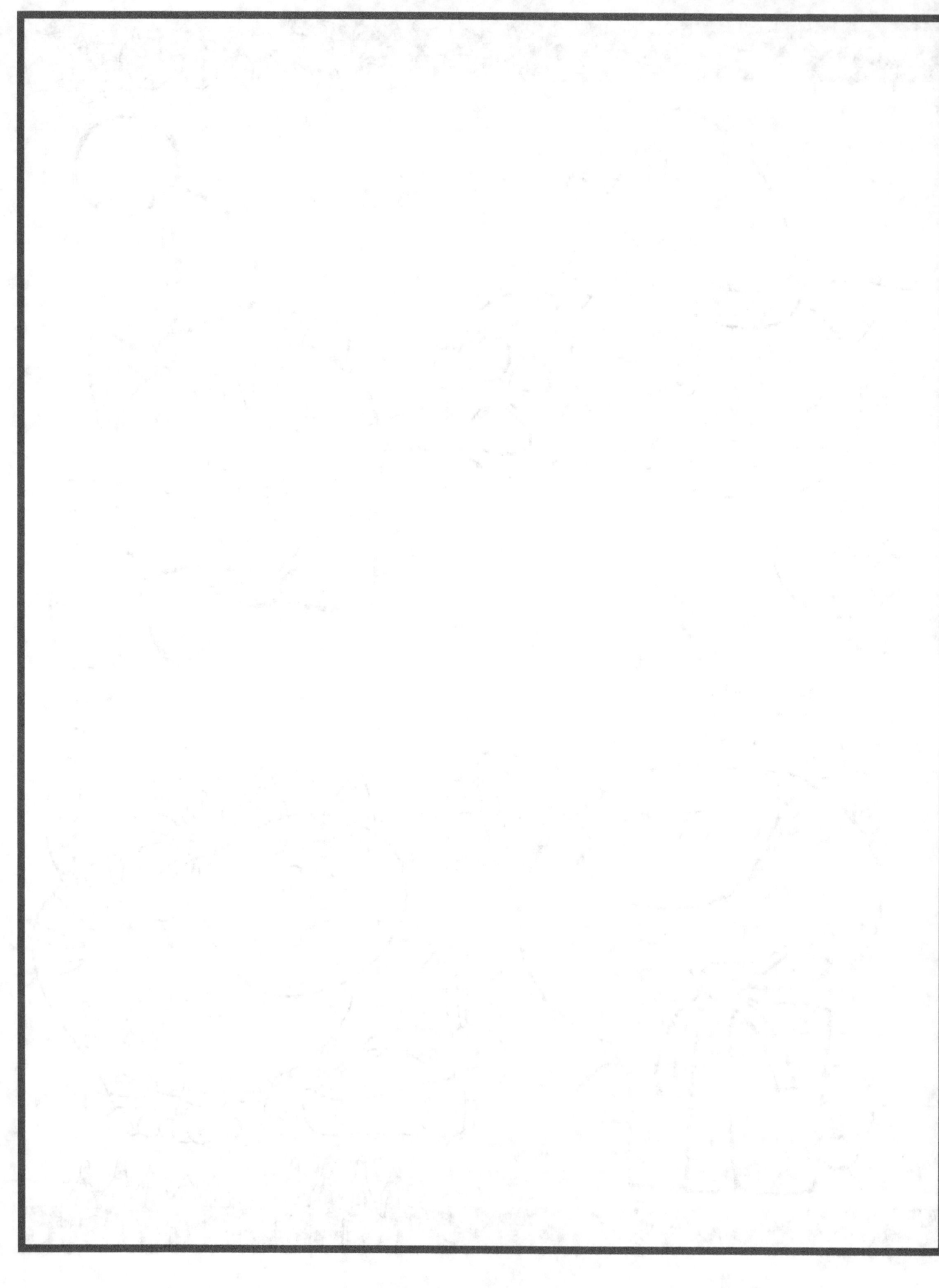

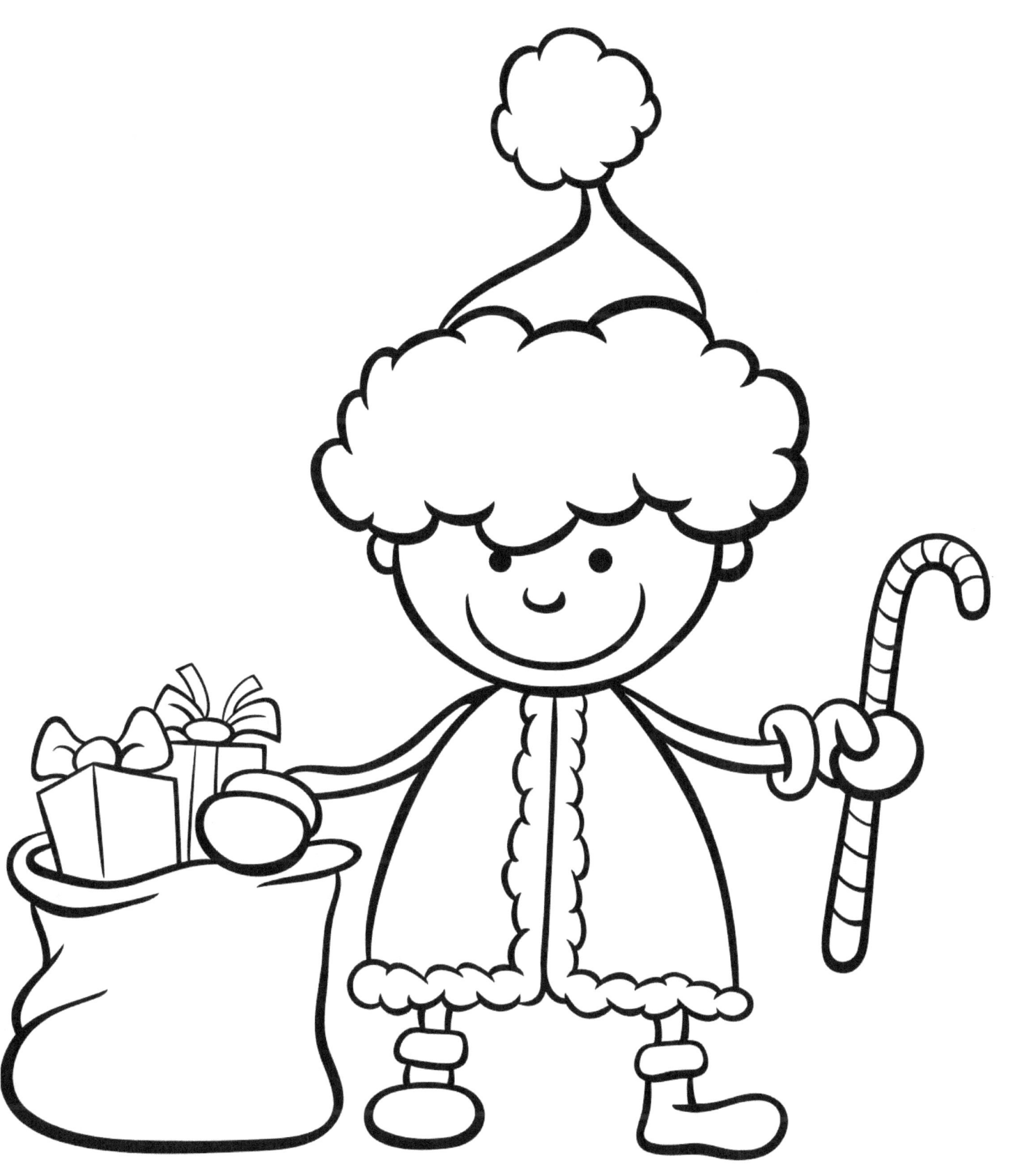

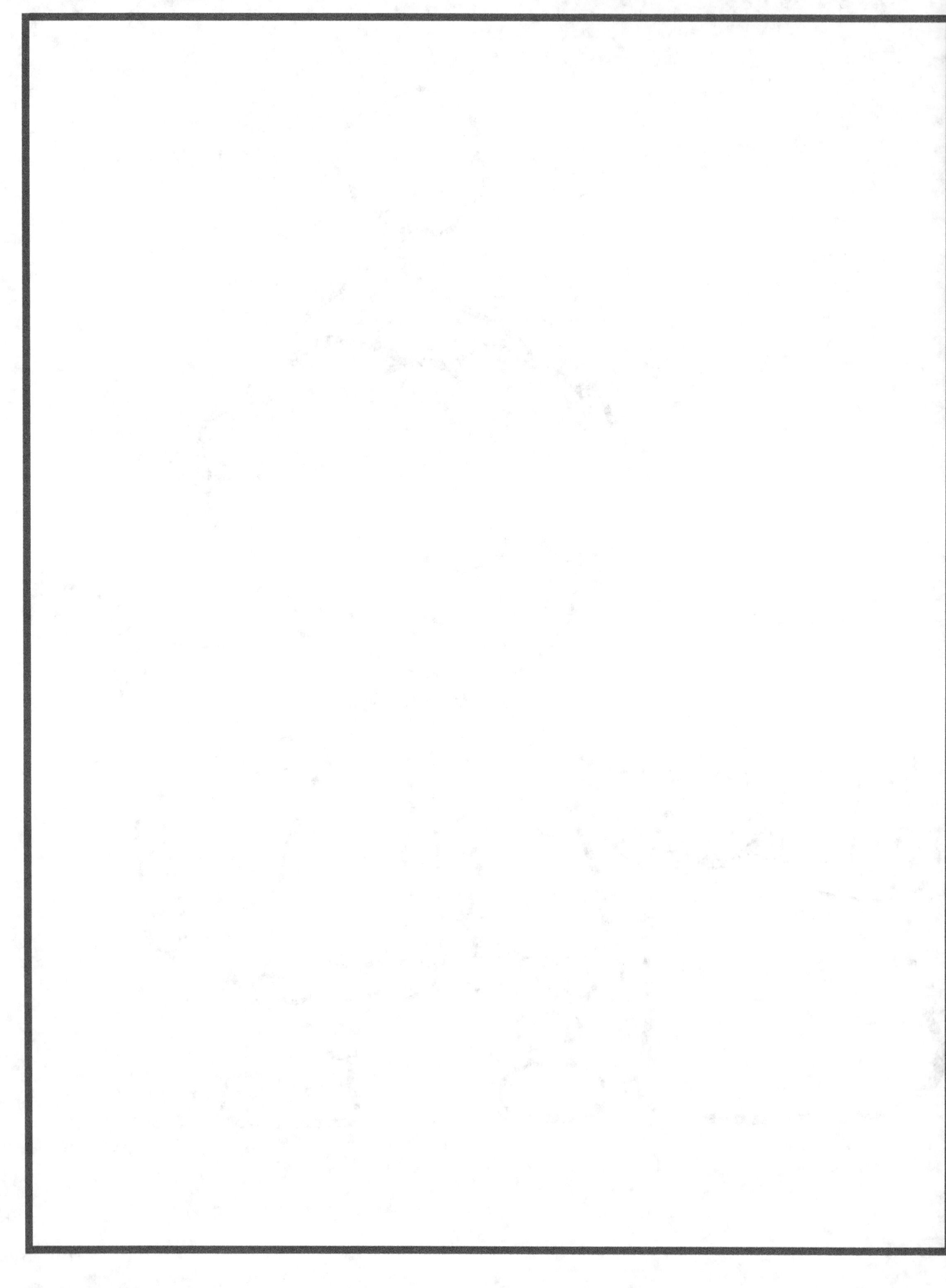

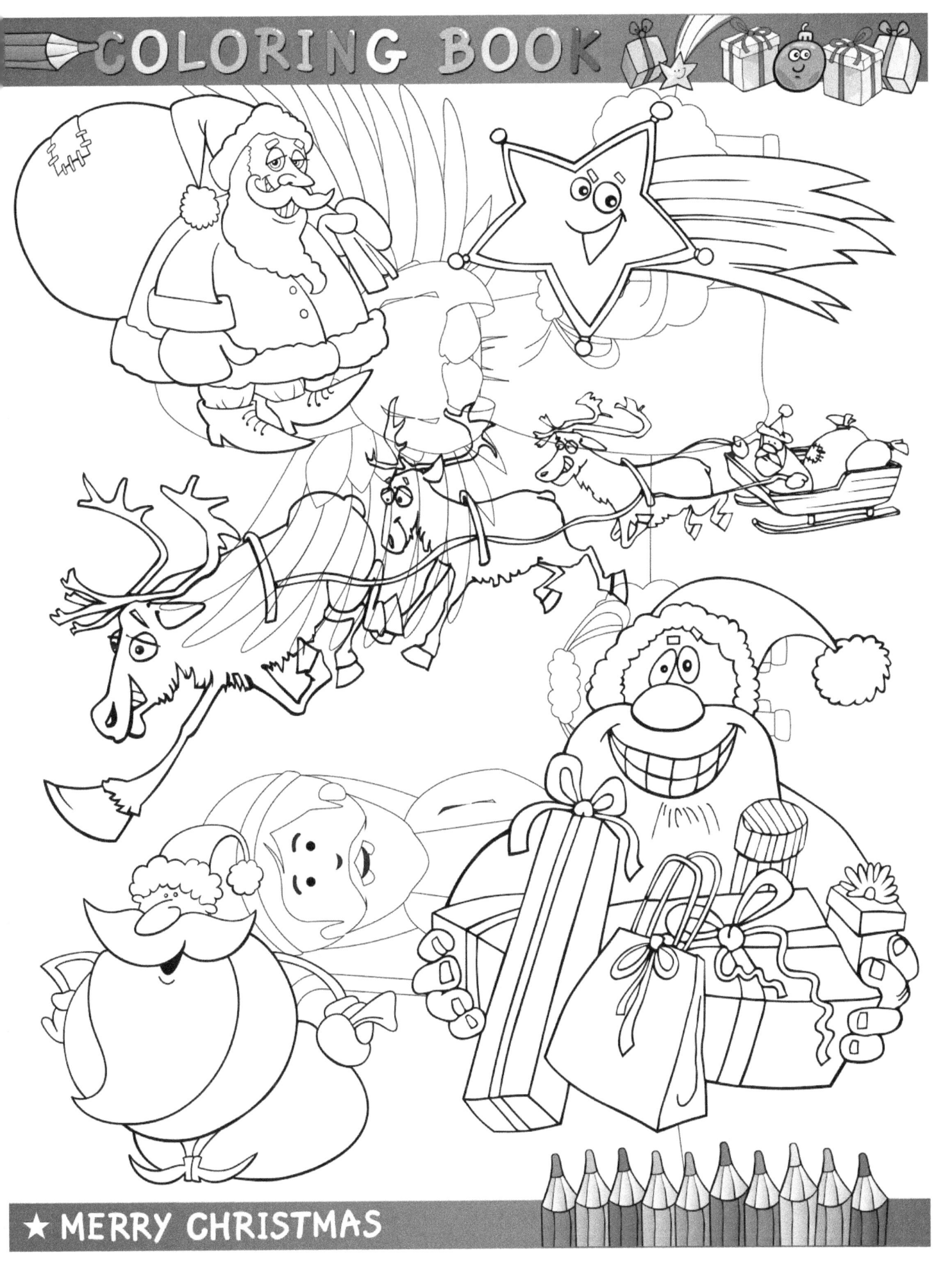

COLORING BOOK

★ MERRY CHRISTMAS

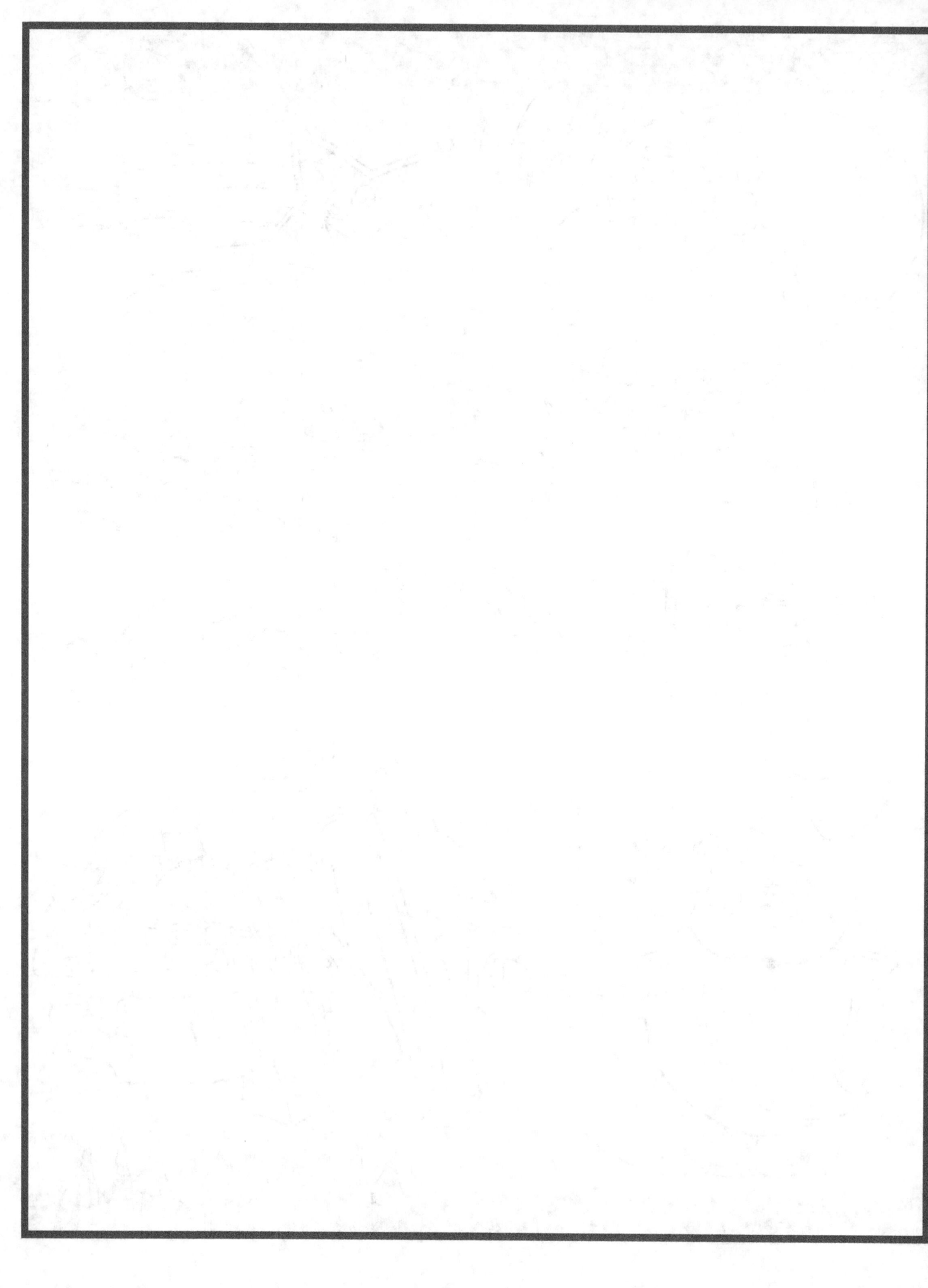

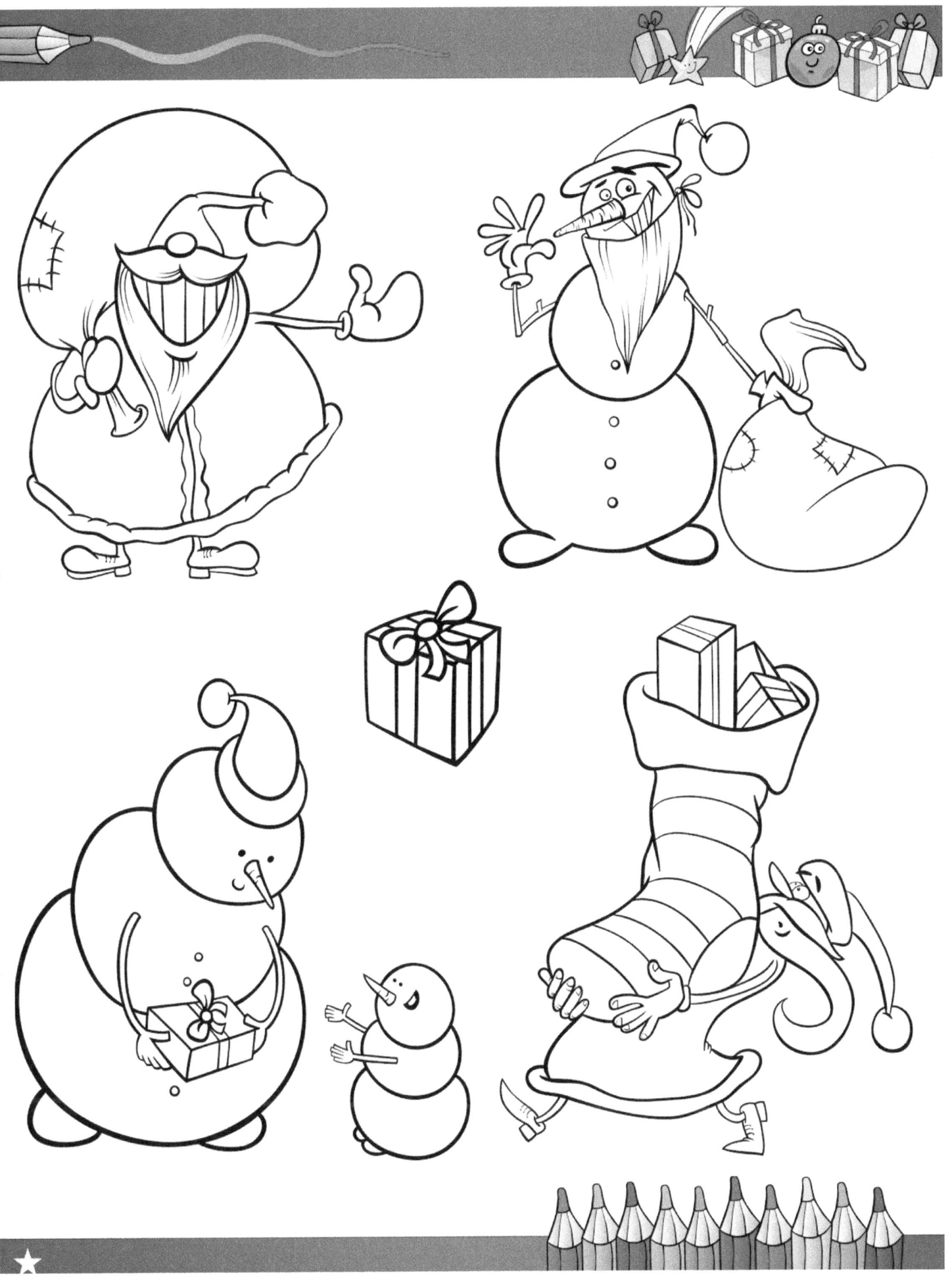

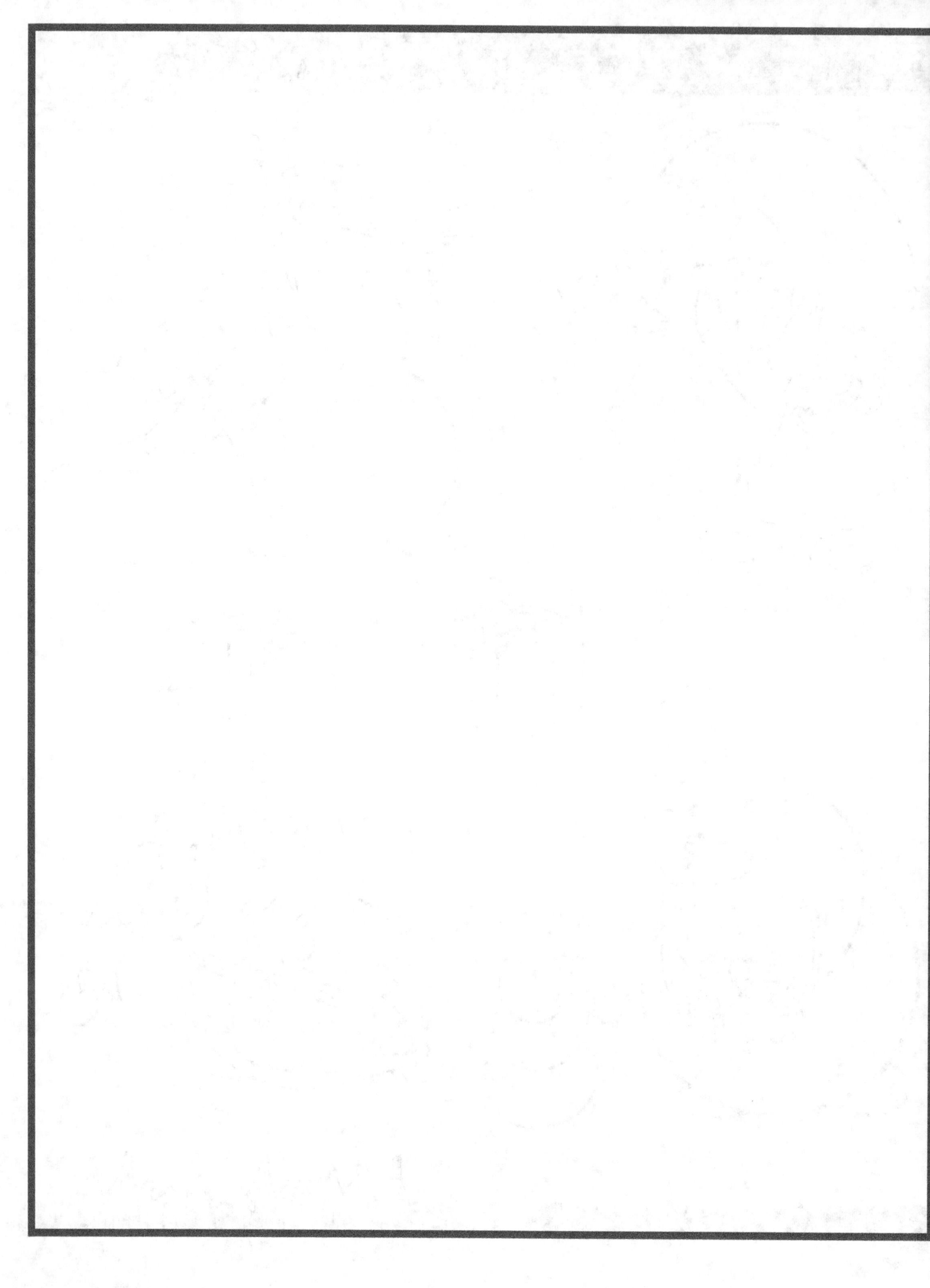

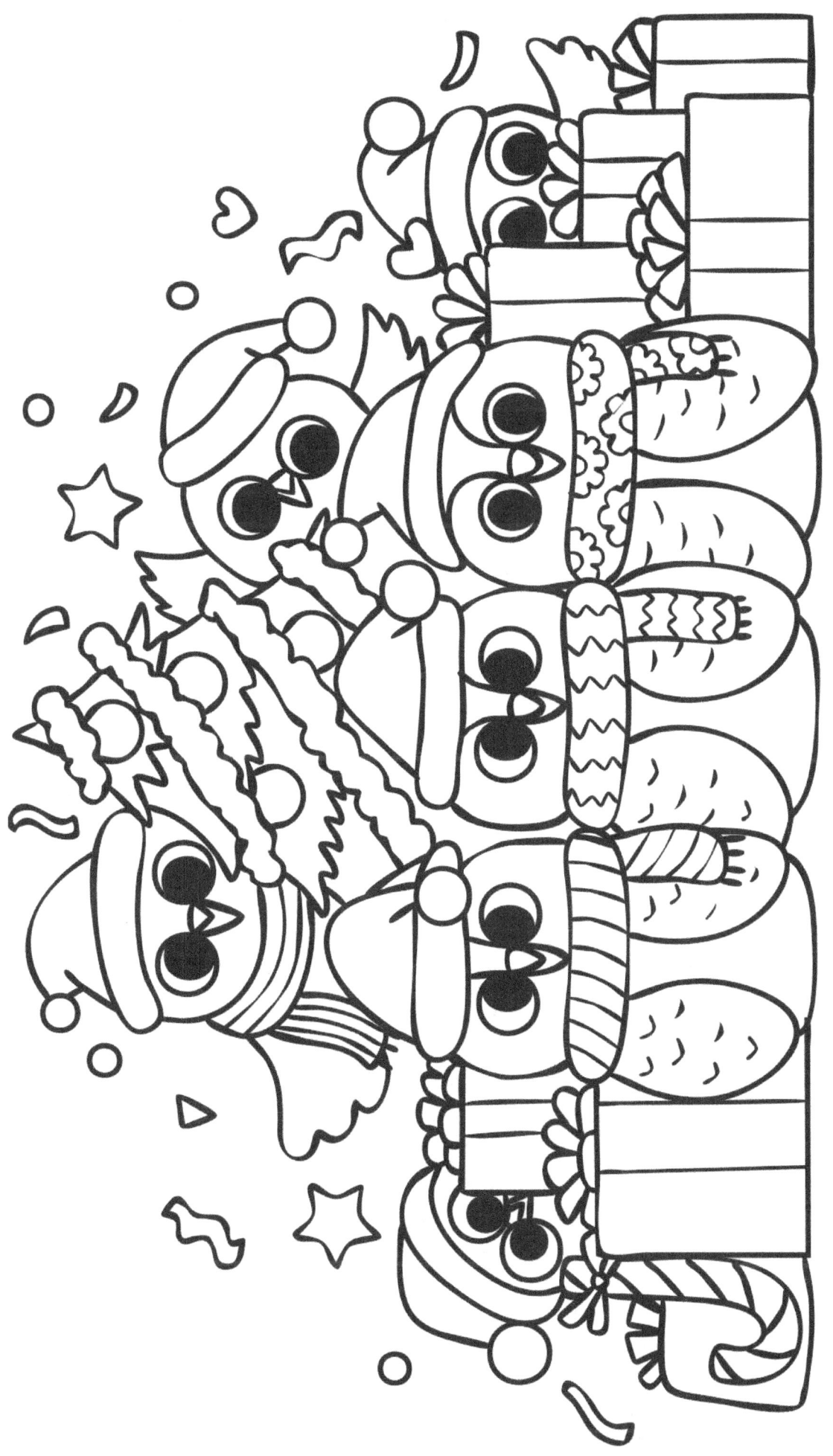

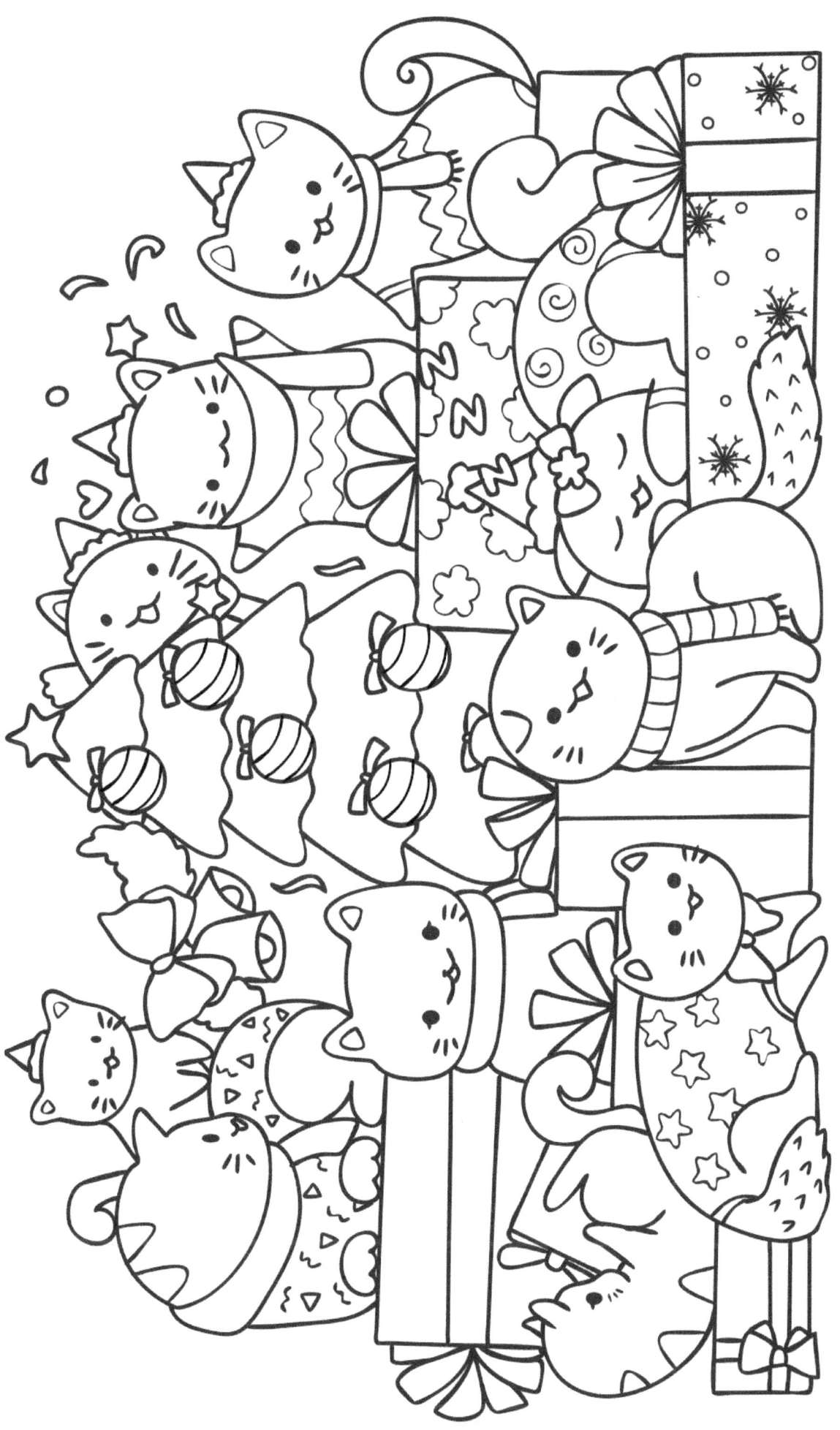

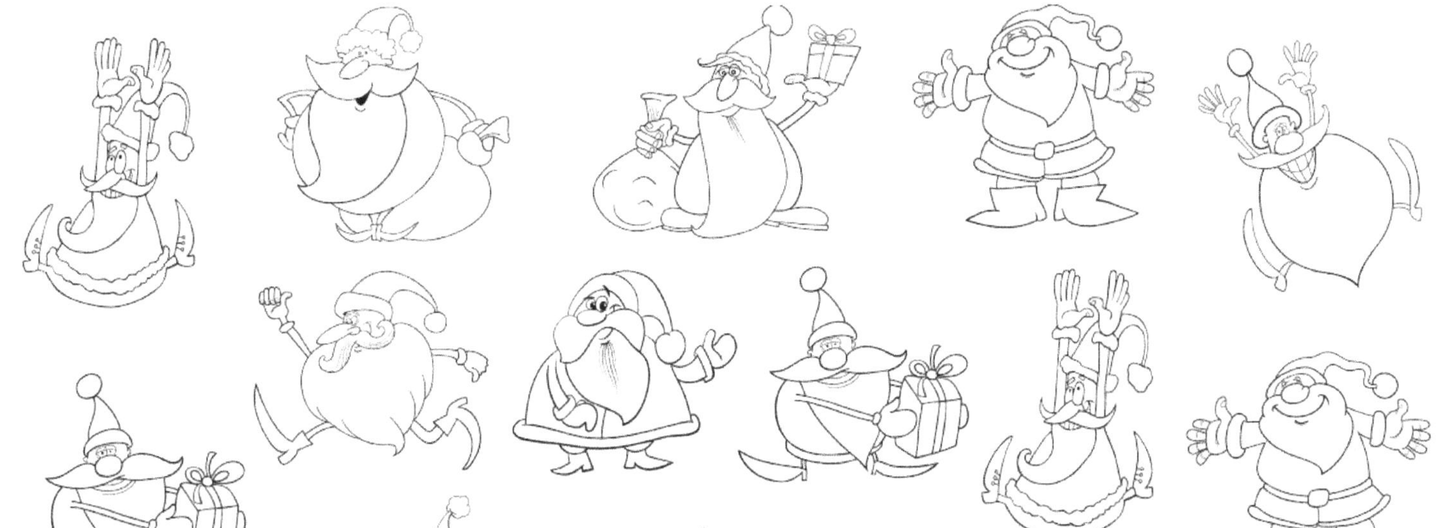

CHRISTMAS

FIND
ONE
OF A KIND

ANSWER

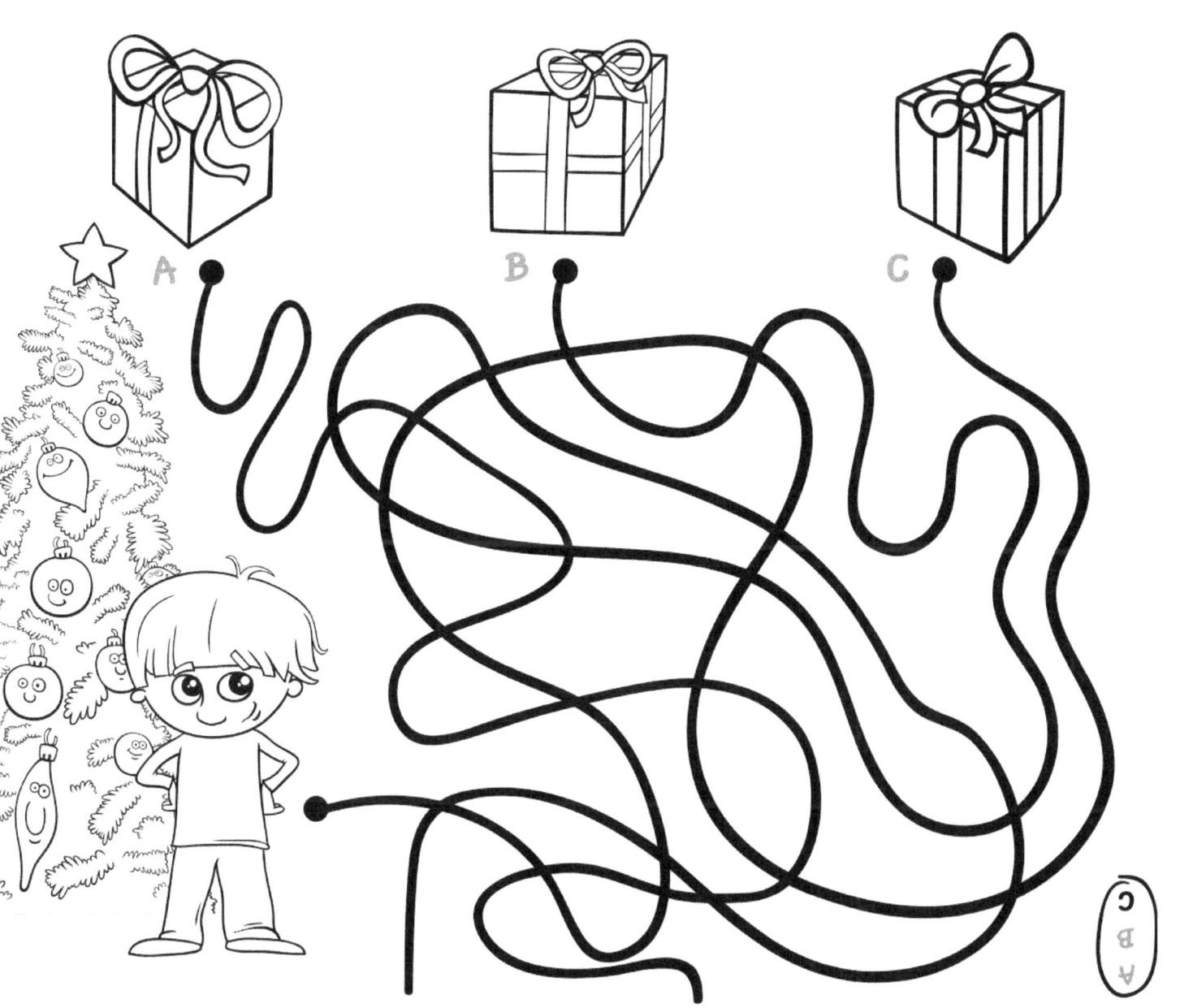

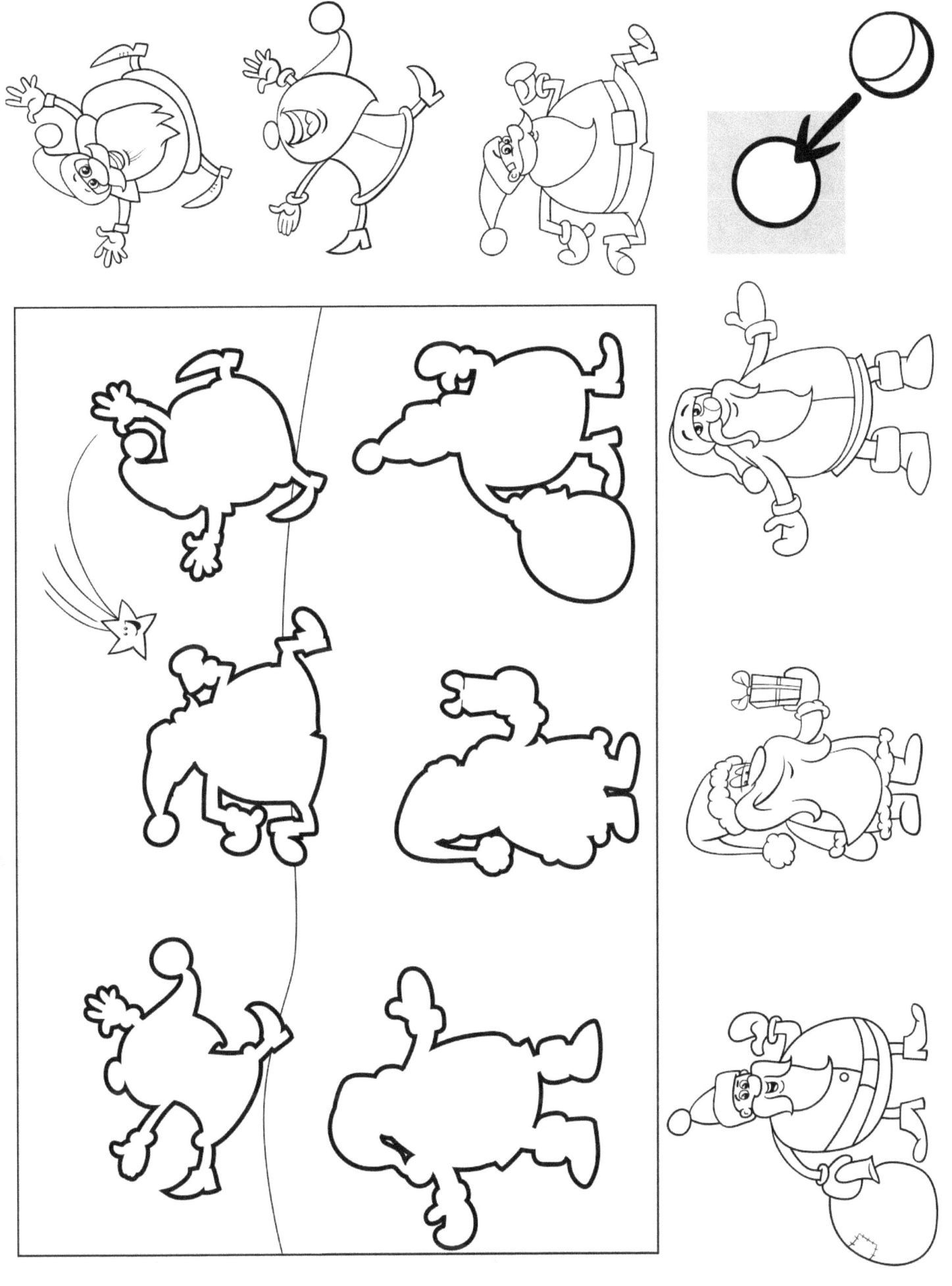

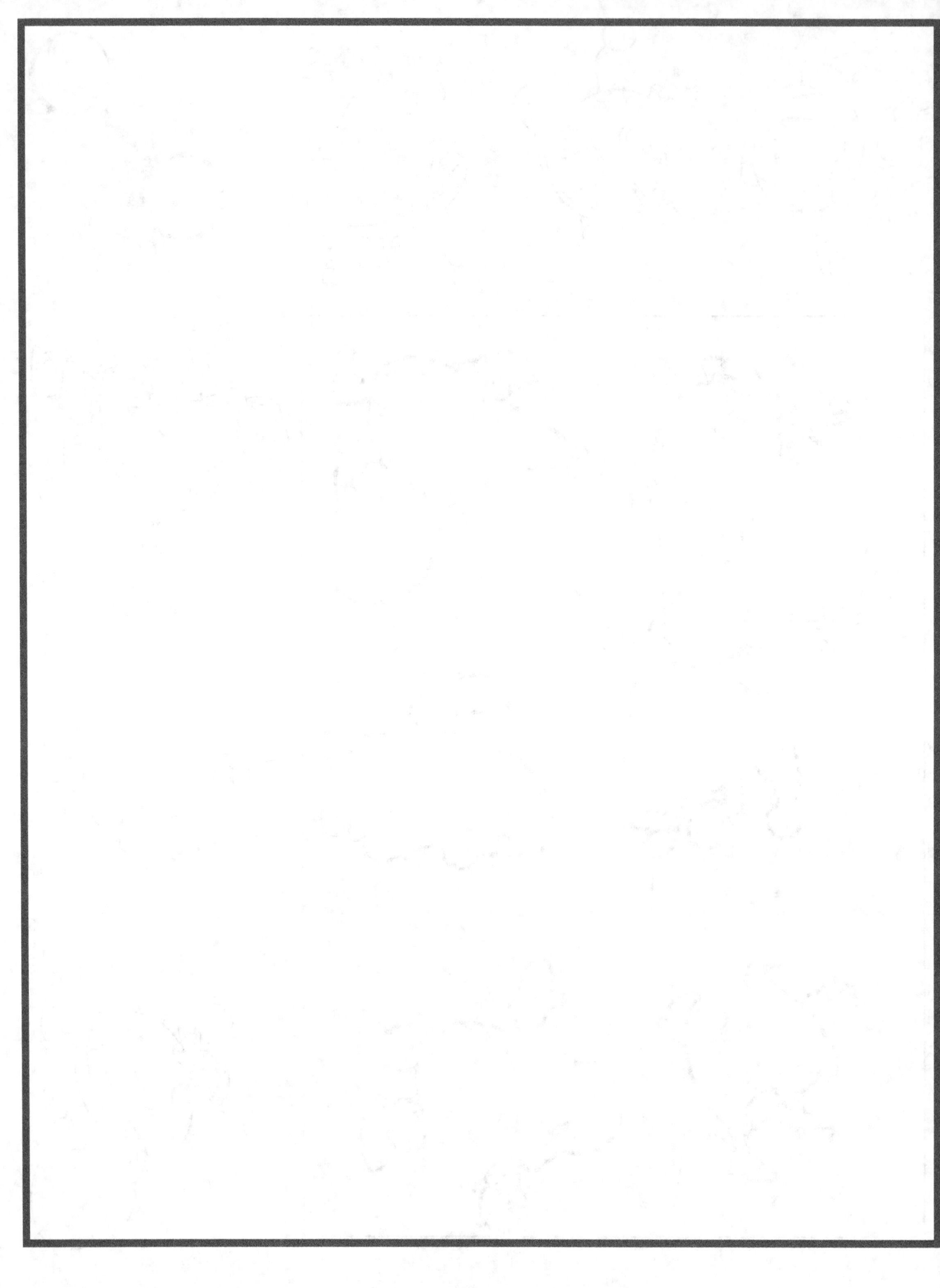

1				
2				
3				
4				

WHAT COMES NEXT?

1

2

3

4

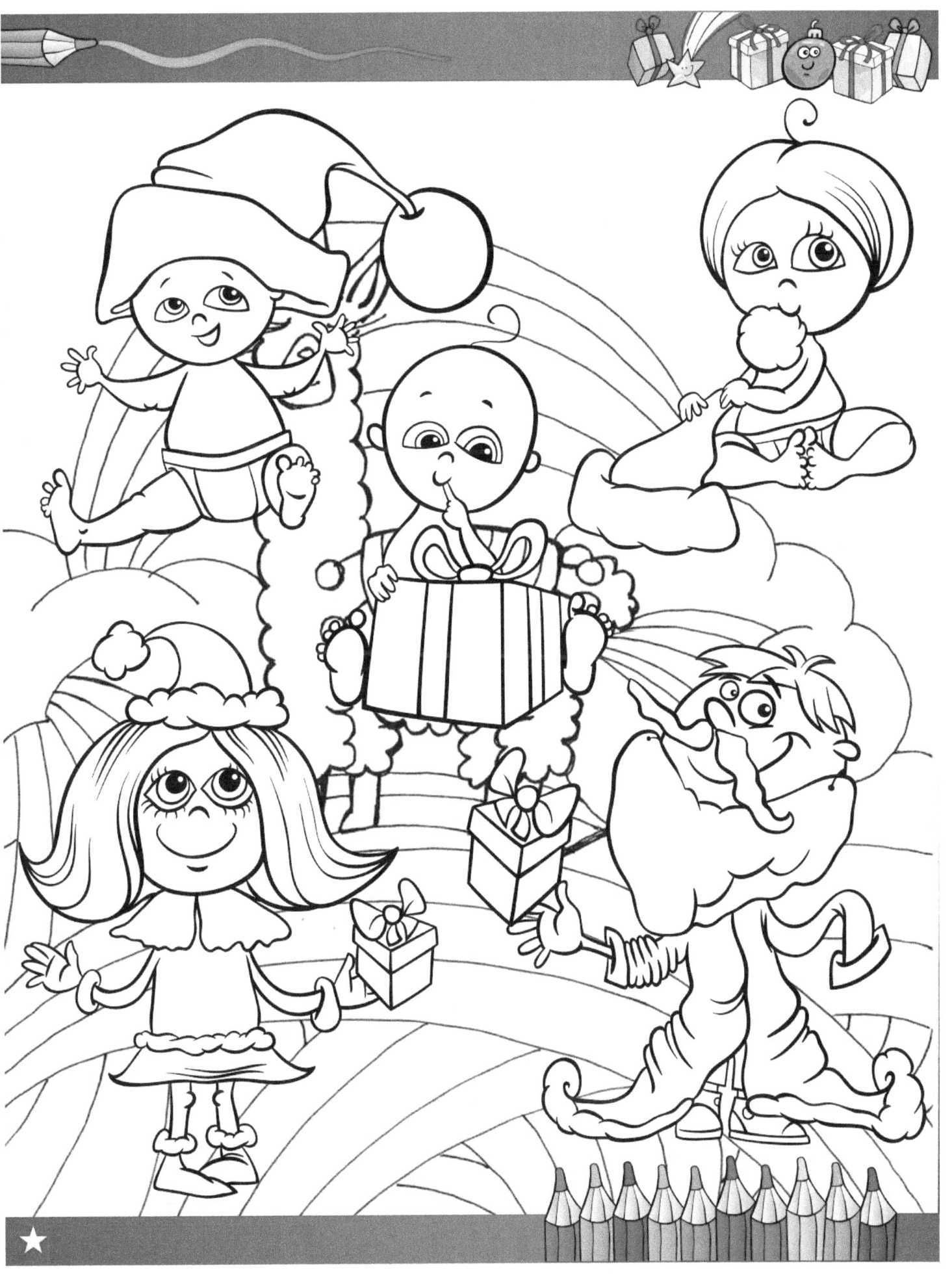

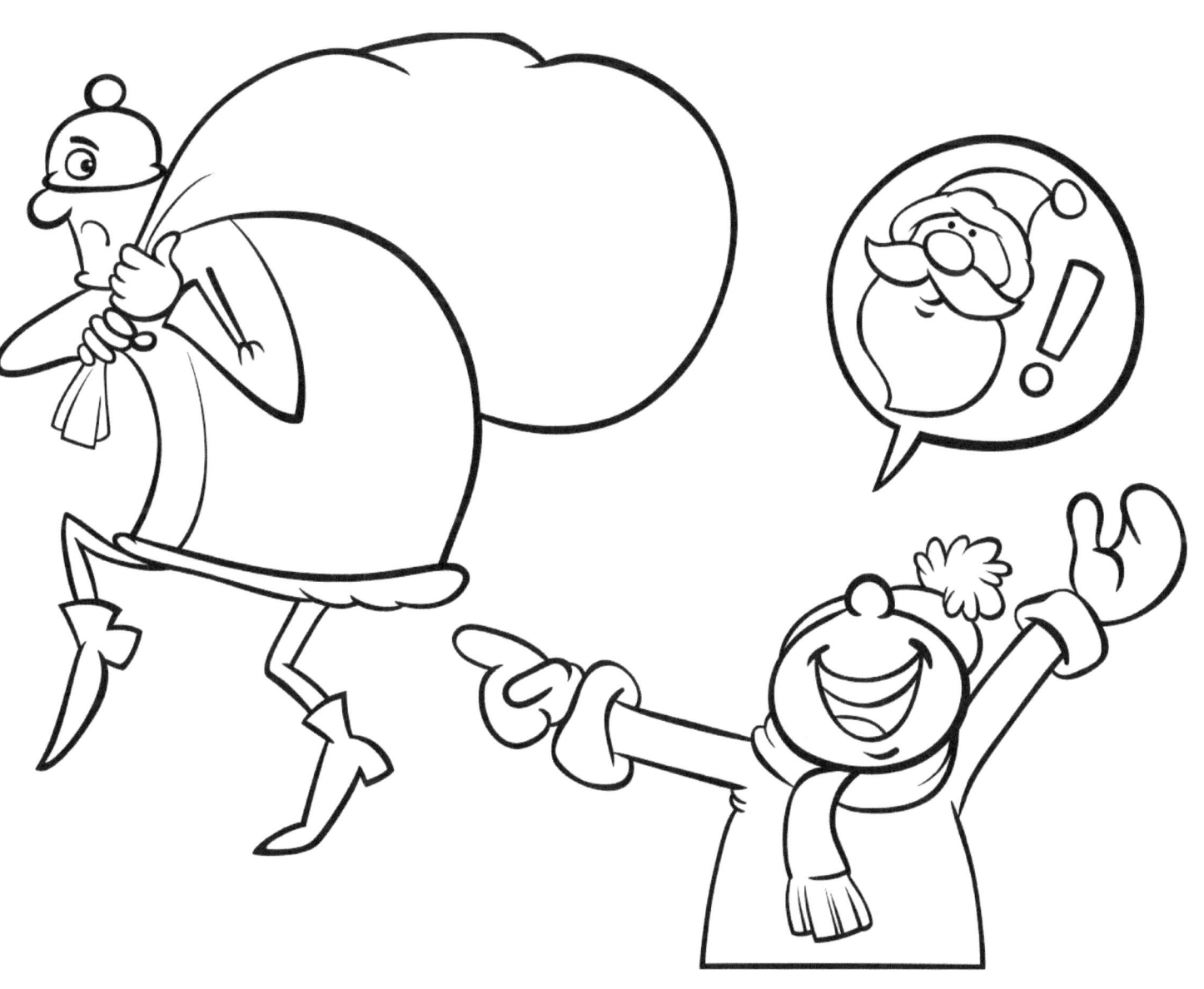

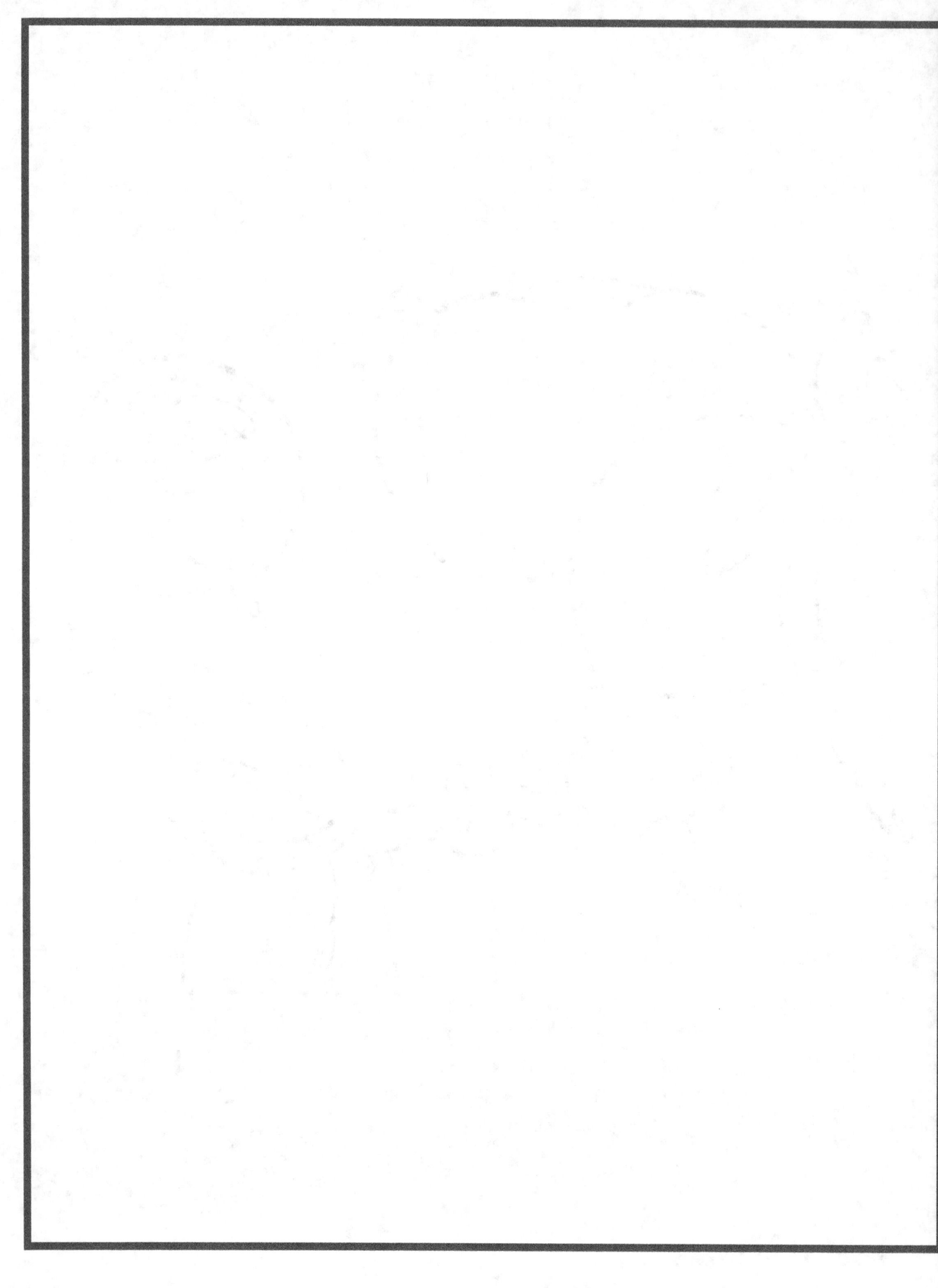

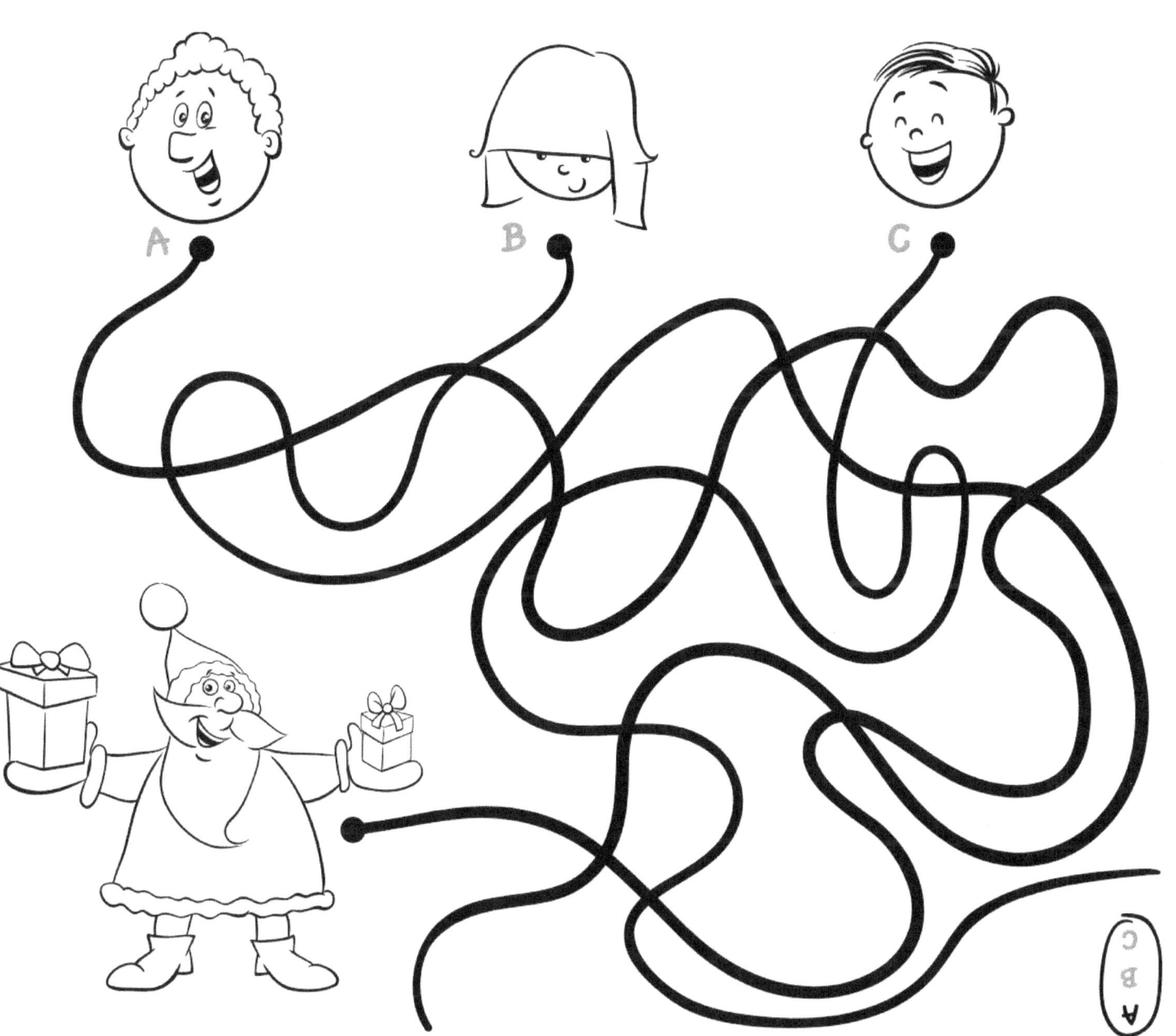

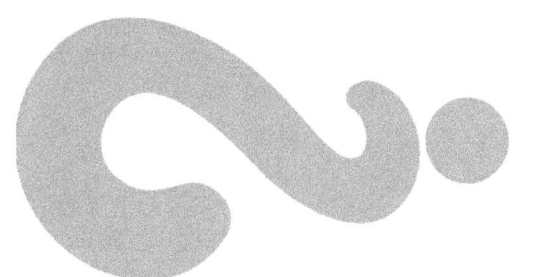

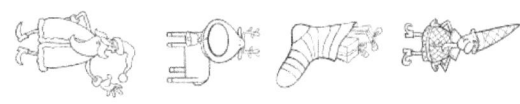

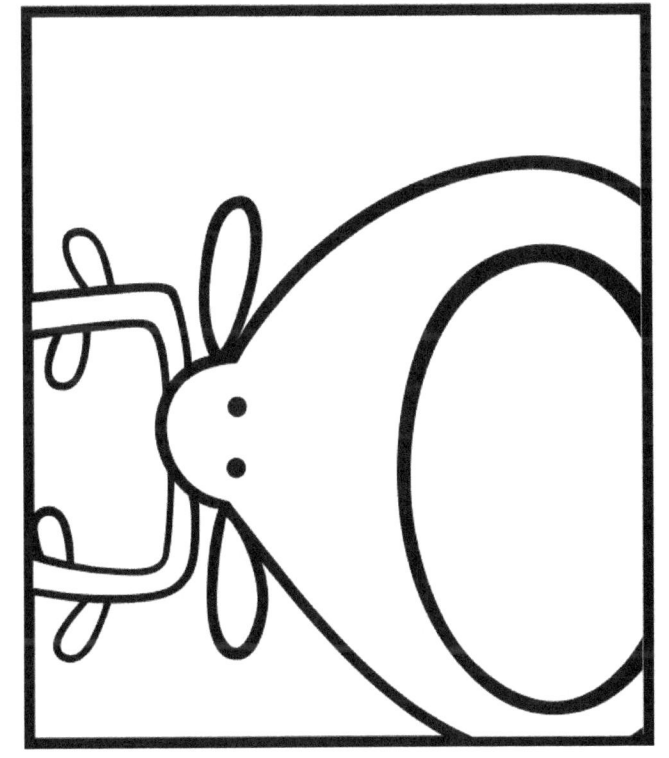

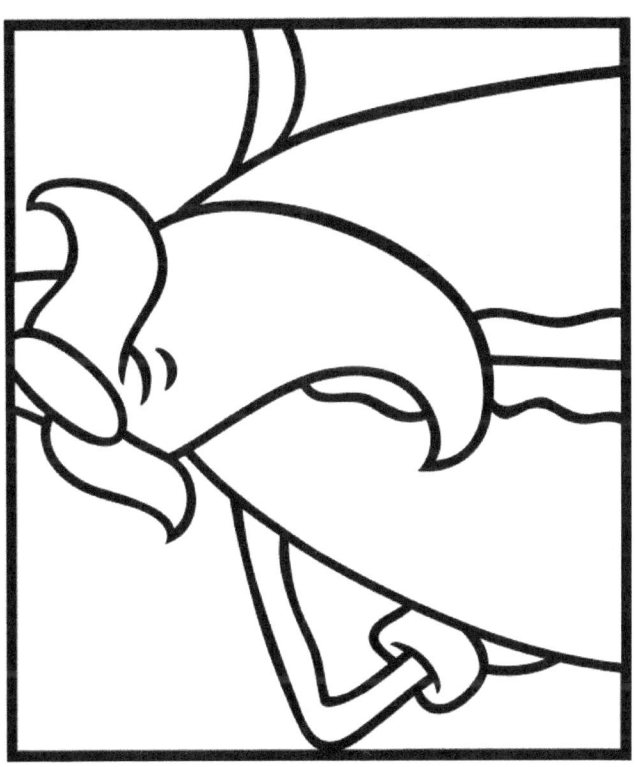

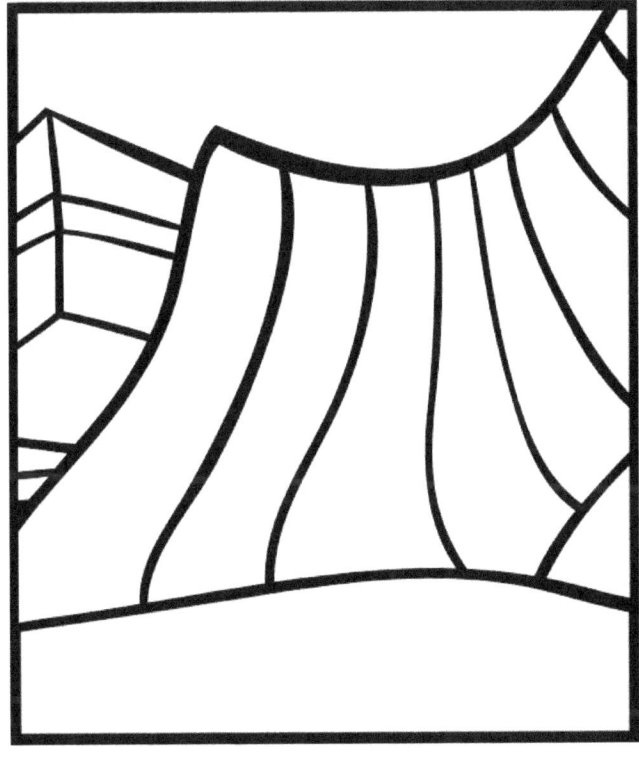

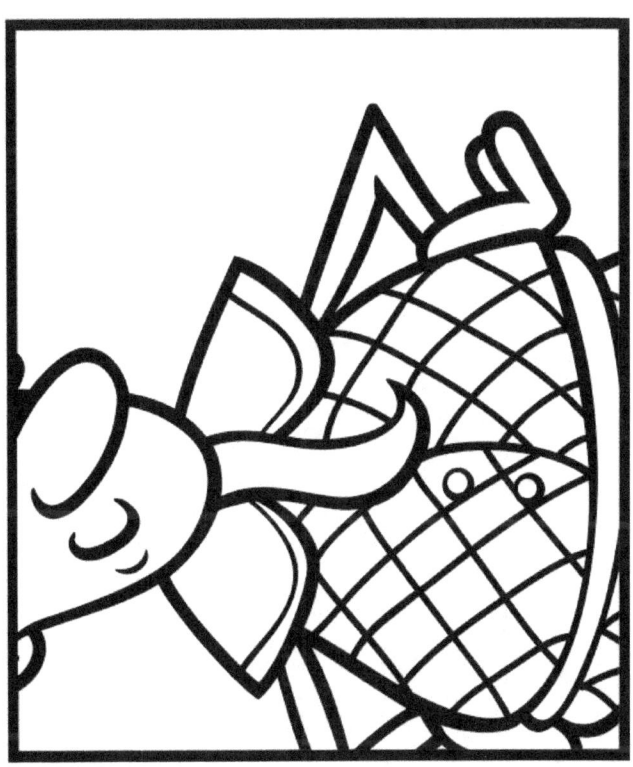

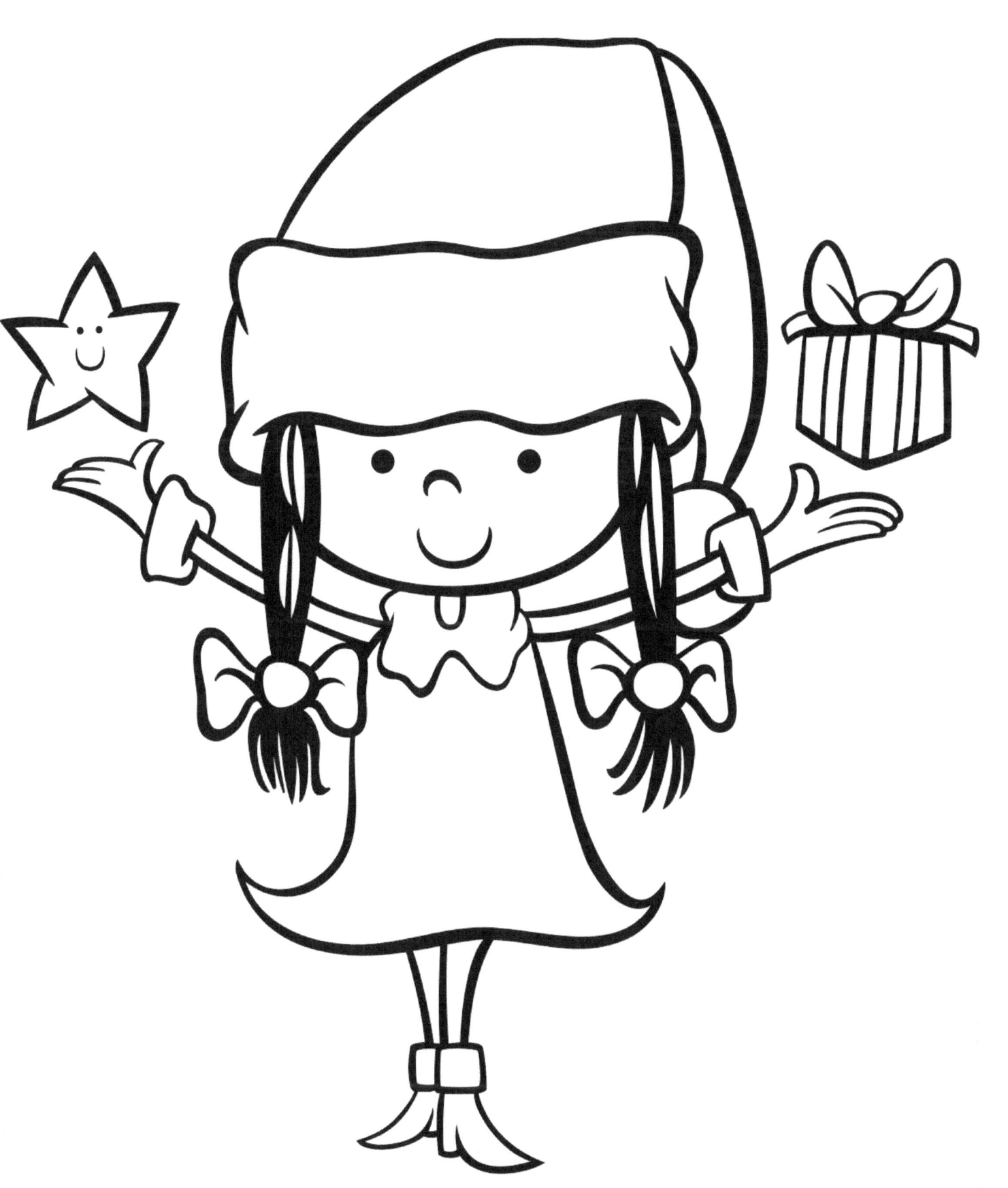

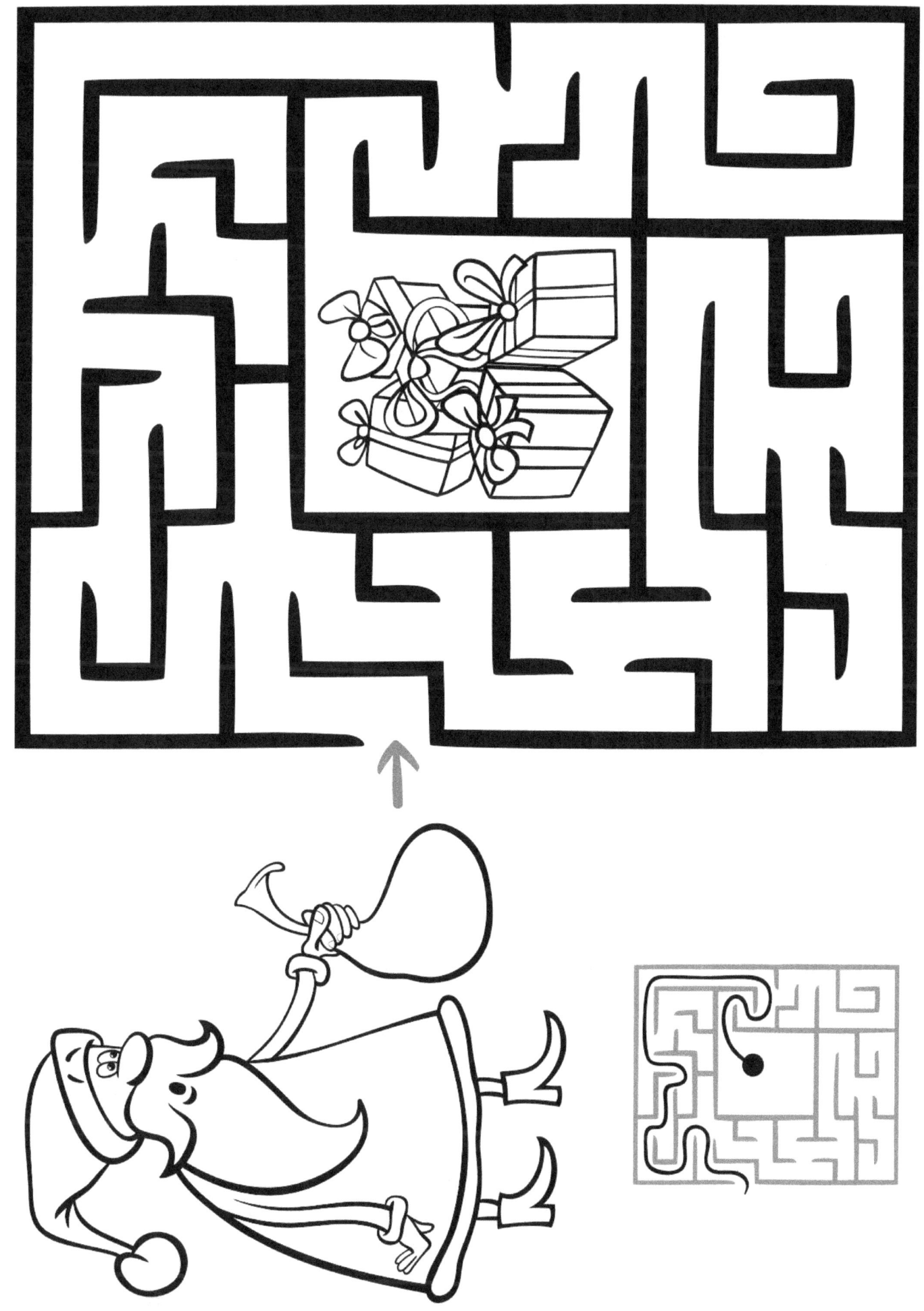

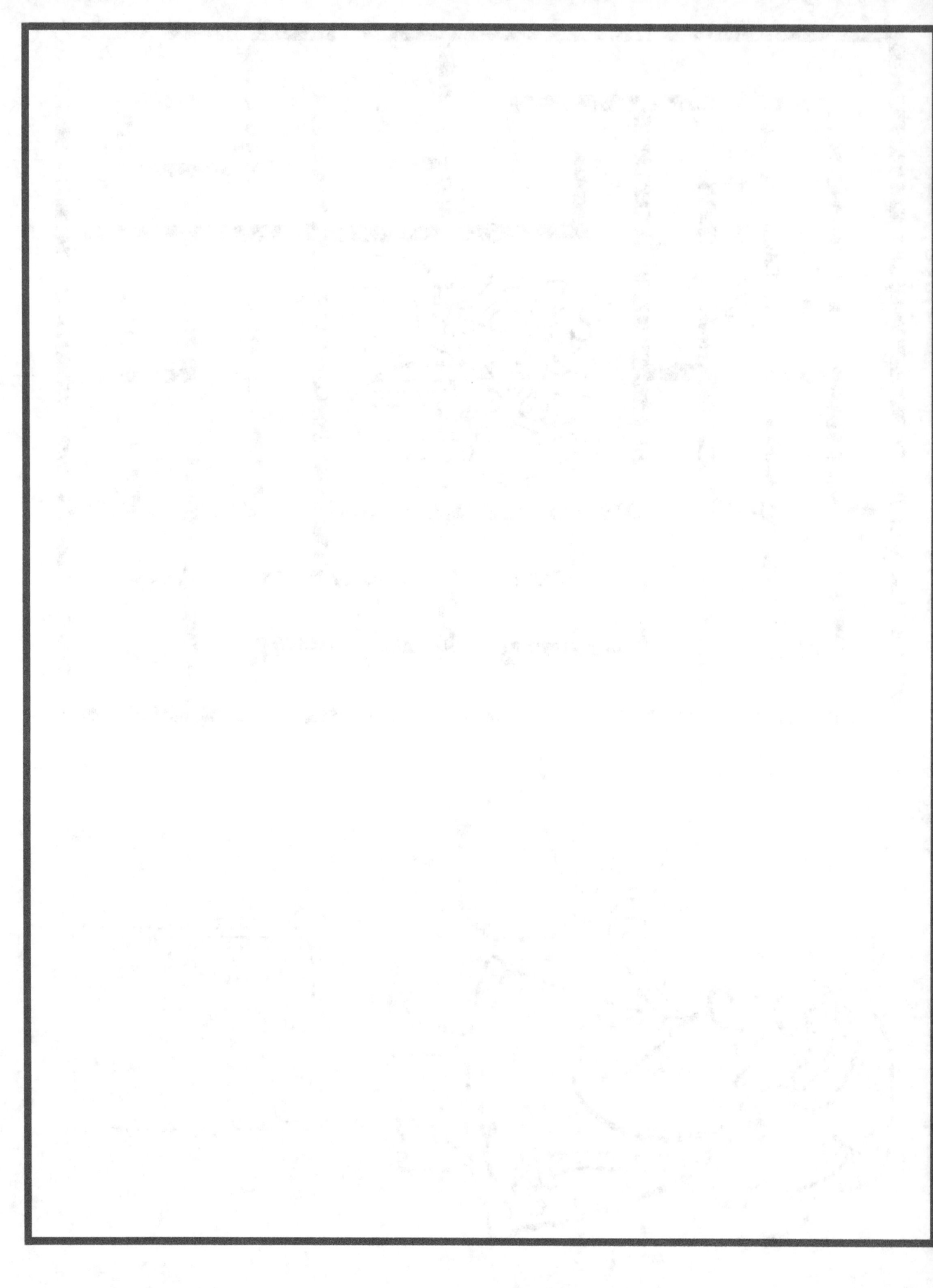

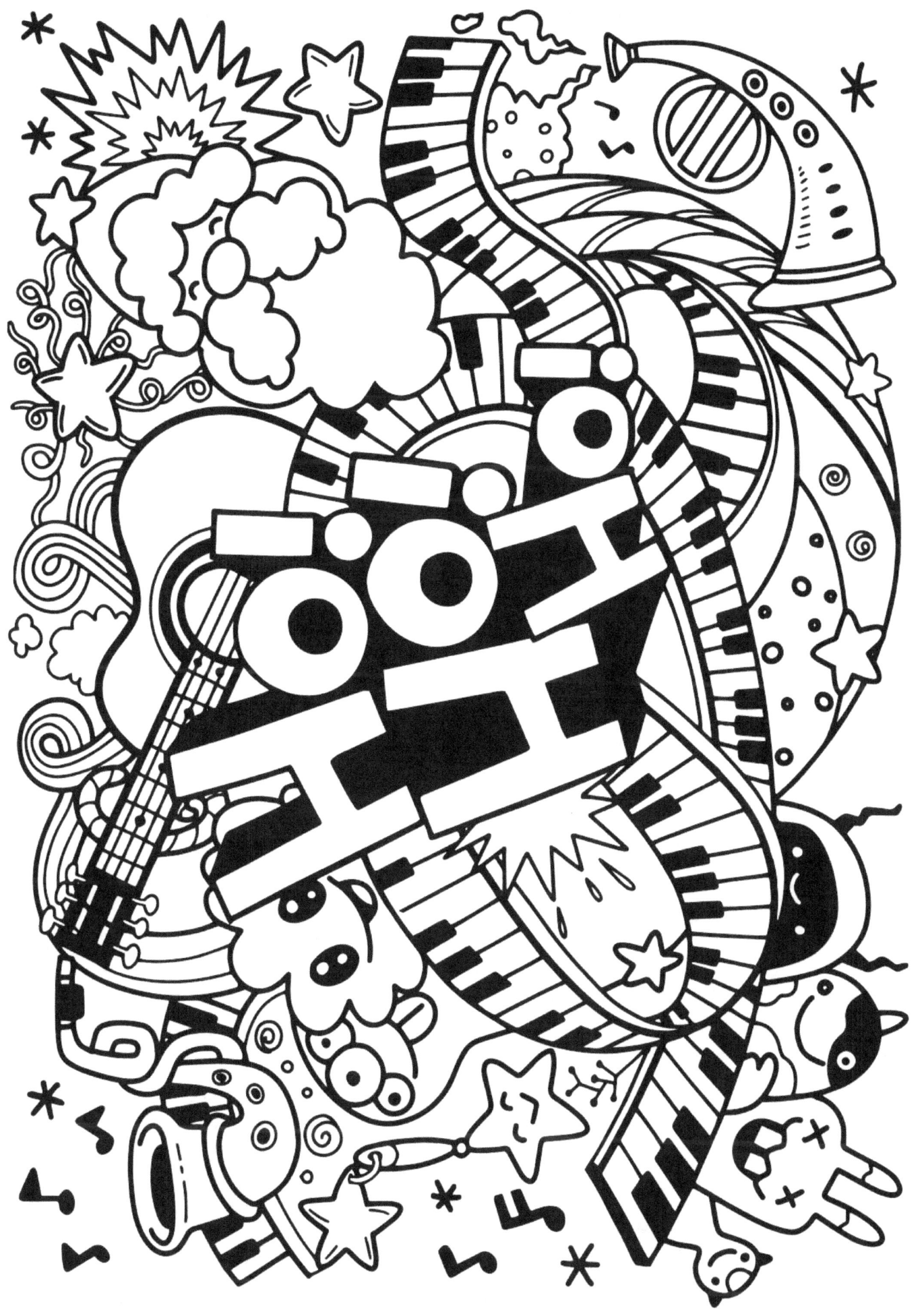

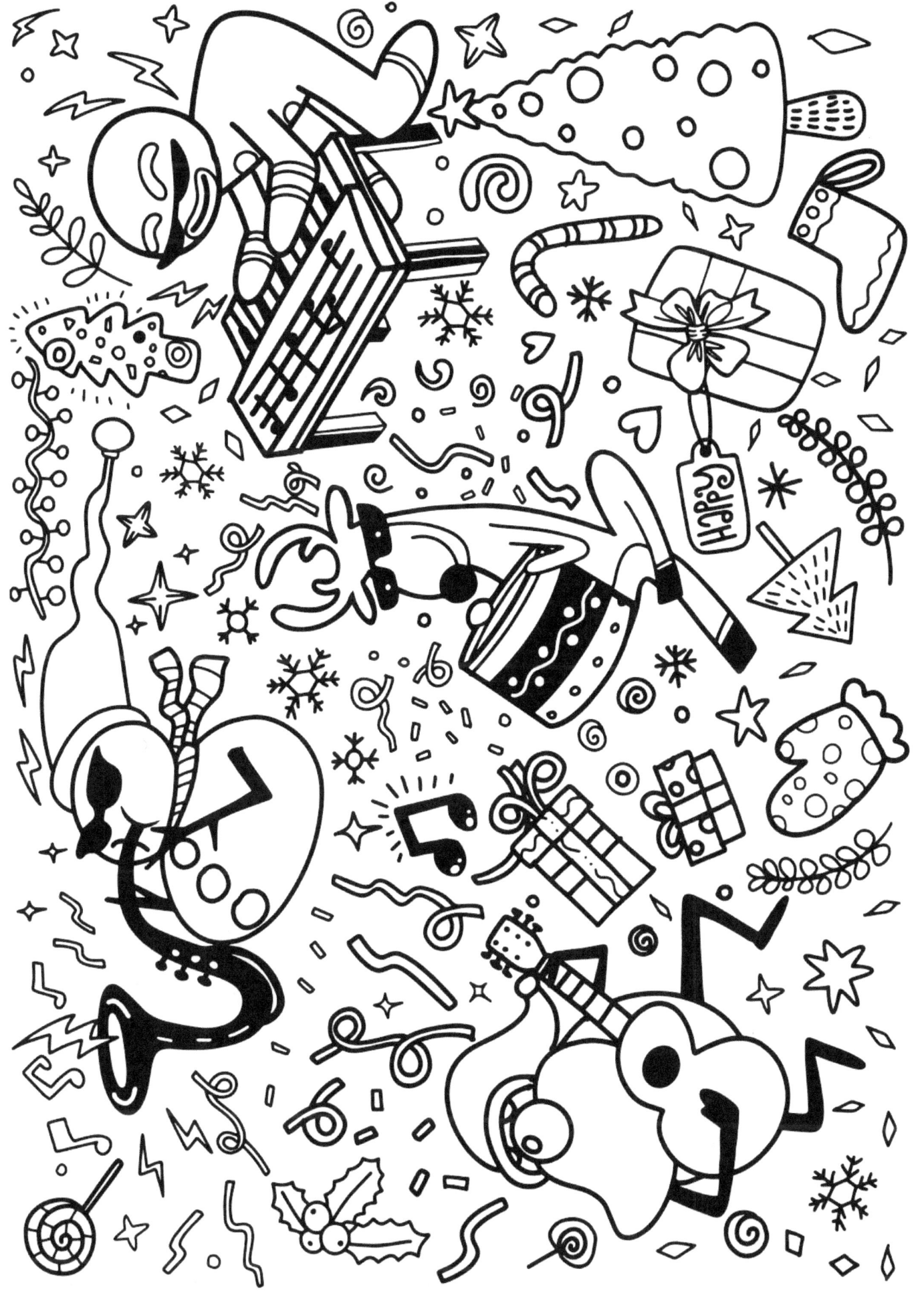

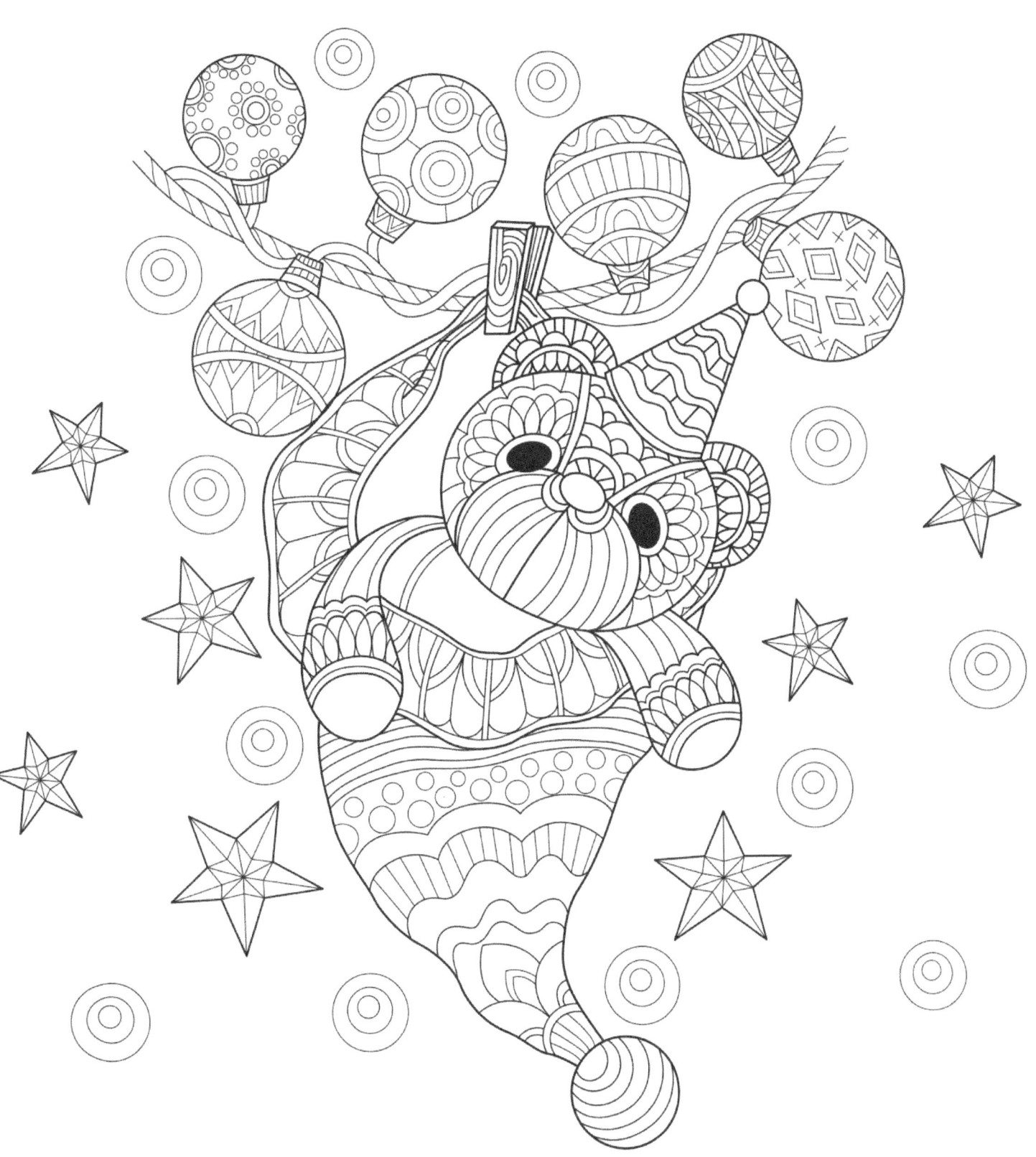

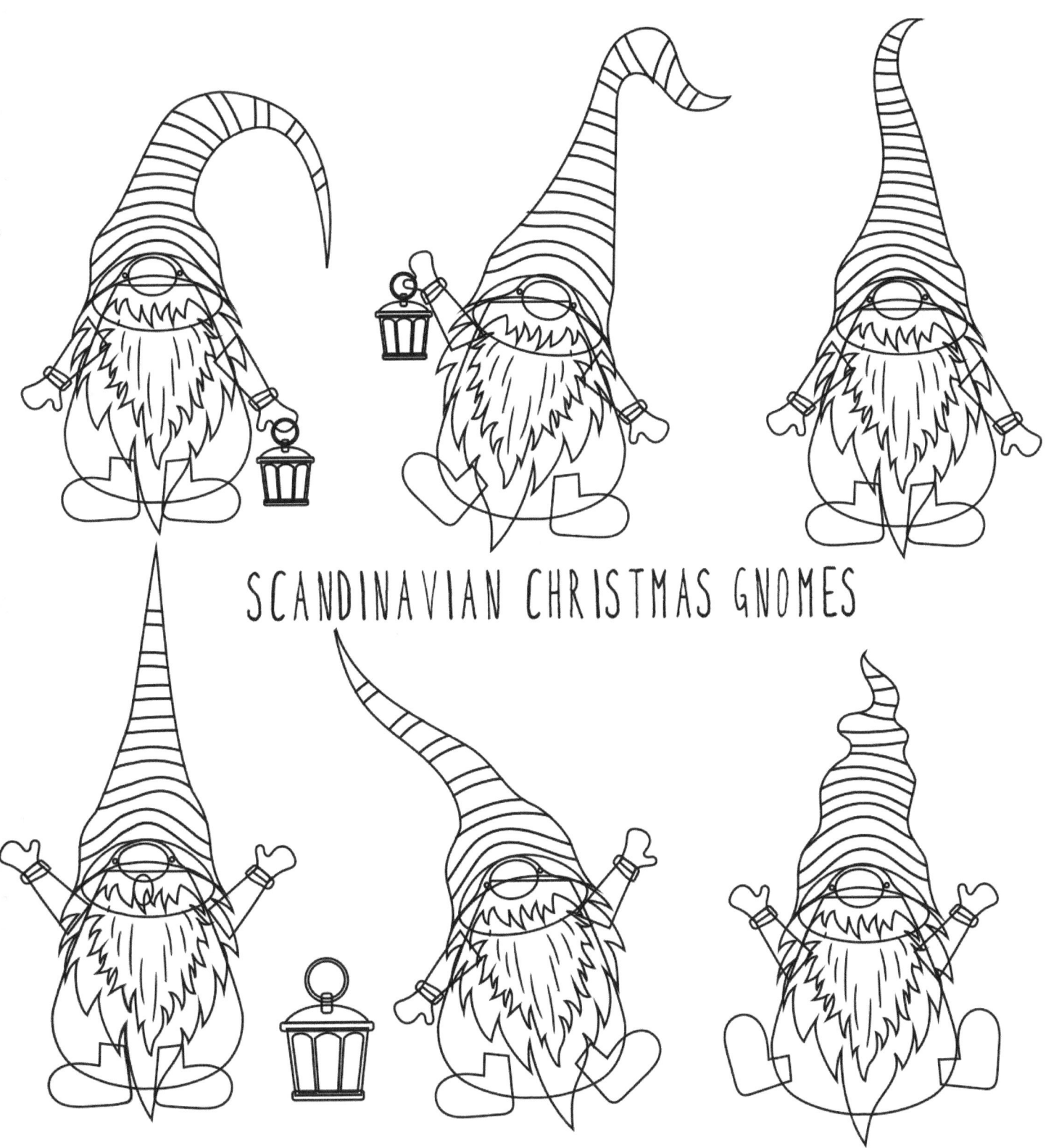

SCANDINAVIAN CHRISTMAS GNOMES

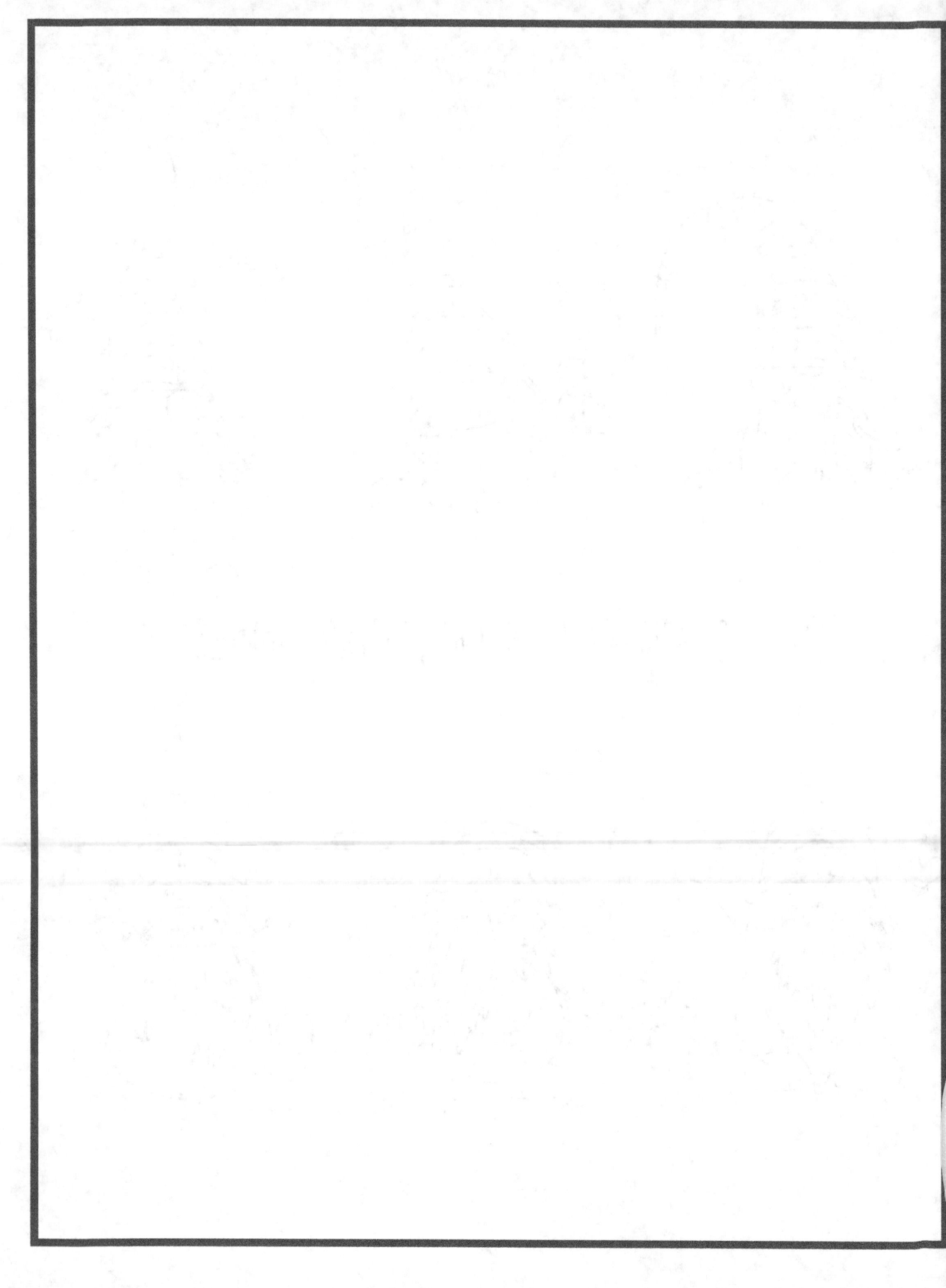

www.ingramcontent.com/pod-product-compliance
Lightning Source LLC
Chambersburg PA
CBHW081544220526

45467CB00010B/3315